WRITING ABOUT MAGIC
Rayne Hall

Copyright Rayne Hall © 2013-2015

All Rights Reserved - content copyright Rayne Hall

Cover Art and Design: Erica Syverson

Scimitar Press, St. Leonards (March 2015 Paperback Edition)

ISBN-13: 978-1508830016

ISBN-10: 1508830010

WRITING ABOUT MAGIC

Rayne Hall

CONTENTS

INTRODUCTION - 8

1. MAGICIAN CHARACTERS - 13
Personality Profile. Food for Thought. Assignment

2. MAGIC SYSTEMS - 21
Pick a System. High Magic and Low Magic. Black Magic and White Magic. Ceremonial Magic. Natural Magic. Religious Magic. Alchemy. Traditional Witchcraft. Wiccan Witchcraft. Necromancy. Shamanism. Ancient Egyptian Magic. Folk Magic. Voodoo. Invent a System. Terms, Definitions, Spellings. Blunders to Avoid. Further Reading. Food For Thought. Assignment.

3. TRAINING AND INITIATION - 41
Training Opportunities. School of Magic. Apprenticeship. Self-Study. Part-Time Study Informal Learning. Candidate Selection. The Daily Grind of Learning. Examples from Literature. Initiation. Blunders to Avoid. Food for Thought. Assignment.

4. RITUAL AND POWER-RAISING - 52

Structure of the Ritual. Casting the Circle. Invocation. Altering the State of Consciousness. Raising Power. Speaking the Spell. Dismissing the Spirits. Closing the Circle. Grounding. Keeping Records. Resting. Fiction Ideas for Power-Raising. Blunders to Avoid. Food For Thought. Assignment.

5. LOCATION AND CIRCLE-CASTING -59

Choosing the venue. How to Cast the Circle. Choosing the Time. Plot Possibilities. Food for Thought. Assignment.

6. COSTUMING AND EQUIPMENT -65

What the Magician Wears. Equipment. Plot Possibilities. Further Reading Food for Thought. Assignment.

7. PHRASING THE SPELL - 70

How to Write A Spell. Sample Spells. Further Reading. Food for Thought. Assignment.

8. CORRESPONDENCES - 75

Using Charts. Correspondence Topics. List of Colour Correspondences. Further Reading. Food for Thought. Assignment.

9. LOVE SPELLS - 81

Rituals. Clients. Conflicts. Does Your Magician Perform Love Spells? Conflict - Plot Possibilities. Consequences - Plot Possibilities. Further Reading. Food for Thought. Assignment.

10. SEX MAGIC - 89

Power-Raising. Structure of the Ritual. Variations. Plot Possibilities. Further Reading. Assignment.

11. MAGICAL WEAPONS AND WARFARE - 94

Material, Size and Shape. How it Works. Charging and Cleansing. Plot Possibilities. How to Defeat a Magician. Magic in Warfare. Assignment.

12. HEALING AND PROTECTION - 102

Healing. Protection. Guarding Against Harmful Magic. Hexes and Curses. Protection Against Magical Attacks. Talismans and Amulets. Further Reading. Food for Thought. Assignment.

13. ETHICS, CONFLICTS, SECRECY - 112

Ethics. Villainous Ethics. The Wiccan Rede. Secrecy. When Mages Make Mistakes - Plot Possibilities. Outer Conflict - Plot Possibilities. Inner Conflict - Plot Possibilities. Food for Thought. Assignment.

14. ILLUSIONISTS AND CHARLATANS - 126

Illusionists. What They Do. How It's Done. Psychological Profile of an Illusionist. Charlatans. Psychological Profile of a Charlatan. Religious Charlatans. Blurred Lines. Plot Possibilities. Assignment.

15. MAGIC IN THE FUTURE - 134

Future Magic Scenarios. Food for Thought. Assignment.

16. FICTION SAMPLES - 138

Short story 'By Your Own Free Will'. Excerpt from Storm Dancer.

FURTHER READING - 173

Useful books for further research.

INTRODUCTION

Tales of magic enchant. Since the earliest days, people have loved to hear about good and evil witches, resourceful shamans, clever wizards and wicked sorcerers, about miracles, curses, love potions and magic swords.

In the modern world, stories about magic continue to weave their spell. Authors like J.R.R. Tolkien, Gabriel García Márquez, Otfried Preußler, Robin McKinley, J.K. Rowling, Shanna Swendson and Jim Butcher have become famous for novels featuring magic.

Magic can enrich fiction in most genres, especially urban fantasy, high fantasy, magical realism, horror, historical fiction and paranormal romance.

To enthral the reader, fictional magic needs to be believable and exciting.

Novice writers may say, "Magic isn't real, therefore I can make up anything and it doesn't matter" - but that attitude leads to unconvincing stories. If you want your readers to suspend their disbelief while they read, you need to suspend yours while you write. You must believe in magic the same way you believe in your characters and in the world you have created.

Magic is a natural force - like gravity, electricity, photosynthesis or evolution - and it has its own laws. Of course, there are different ways to harness this force, and this is where you can use your imagination. Make sure your fictional magic follows the natural laws, then have fun inventing uses and traditions.

If you're a sceptic, struggling to suspend your disbelief, it may help to remember that most people in the history of humankind have believed in magic, and that all civilisations and cultures had ways to harness its power. Only in our modern western society do people think that magic does not exist.

In the modern western world, everyone believes that electricity is real and knows the basics of how it works. In ancient Egypt, everyone believed that magic was real and knew the basics of how it worked.

Imagine time-travelling to ancient Greece and telling the people about this natural power that can be captured, created, sent through thin wires across long distances, and made to turn night into day, silence into music, and cold into warmth. When you tell them about strip lighting, telephones, television, CD players, the internet, carts moving without being pulled by animals and other inventions of the past three hundred years, the good folks will laugh at how gullible you are, or pity your for your madness - or they may whip you out of town for your lies.

Electricity existed in their world and the effects of it were all around them, but they explained these in ways that fit their view of the world. When they saw lightning in the sky, they assumed it was Zeus hurling thunderbolts in anger.

Magic may be all around us even in our modern world, even if we don't understand it, and even if our scientists attribute its effect to other causes. Most people today are as ignorant about magic as the ancient Greeks were about electricity. But in our fiction, magic needs to be as real as electricity, and for this, you must understand how it works. This understanding will open up a whole array of delightful plot possibilities.

Good fiction excites. Many novice writers err by making magic easy; anything can be achieved with magic. The results are unexciting and pointless. If a magician can get anything he wants by saying, "Abracadabra," and solve any problem by pointing his wand, there is no story.

Fortunately, magic has pitfalls and limitations, dangers and dilemmas. Use them, and you'll have a story that thrills.

This book will show you how to create believable magician characters, how to invent magic rituals and compose spells for them, what tools and ingredients they use and how to get them into trouble.

I'll give you lists of plot ideas. Feel free to adapt them for your fiction.

You're the CEO of your fiction; I'm only the consultant. I make suggestions; you choose which of them to apply. Each story is different. If something I advise doesn't suit, simply move on to the next part.

Most chapters are relevant to most stories - but not all. 'Magical Weapons and Warfare' is great for epic fantasy, but probably not for romance. 'Sex Magic' is useful if you write erotica, but if you keep your fiction chaste, this is a chapter to skip.

When talking about characters, I switch between 'she' and 'he'. Almost everything I say applies to either gender.

I write in British English. To the Americans among you some of the words, spellings and grammatical constructions may look odd, but they're correct and I'm sure you'll understand me anyway.

At the end of the book, I've included an excerpt from my fantasy novel *Storm Dancer* and a complete short story, to show how I've used magic in my fiction. Whether or not you enjoy my kind of storytelling and my writing style, you may find it useful to see the theory applied in practice.

Writing About Magic is based on an online course I've taught. It includes an extended version for the lectures as well as additional chapters.

The book is part of the 'Writing Craft' series: *Writing Fight Scenes, Writing Scary Scenes, The Word-Loss Diet, Writing About Villains, Writing About Magic*, with more titles coming soon.

The chapter 'Magical Weapons and Warfare' overlaps with a section from *Writing Fight Scenes.*

This book has only one purpose: to help you write fiction about magic.

If you're looking for guidance on your spiritual path, for an academic analysis of the psychology of magic, for in-depth historical and anthropological research, for hands-on instruction on how to become a magician, or for a quick spell to catapult your novel into the bestseller lists, you need a different kind of book.

However, if you're a fictioneer who wants to write exciting stories about magicians, you've come to the right place.

Rayne Hall

CHAPTER 1: MAGICIAN CHARACTERS

In this chapter you'll create (or refine) the characterisation of your magician.

This may be your novel's heroine, the hero, a minor character or the evil villain, a witch, a ritual wizard, a theurgist, an alchemist, a shaman.... as long as she or he uses magic.

You can use this chapter to deepen the characterisation of a character in a draft or work in progress, or to invent a new character for a future project.

Whatever you decide, it's not set in stone. You can always change it later if your story requires it.

Certain personality traits are common among magicians, and certain talents help them with their craft. Here are some suggestions for characterisation. Your magician should have most - not necessarily all - of these character traits.

PERSONALITY PROFILE

1. Intelligent

Magic requires a sharp intellect, critical thinking, critical analysis and the ability to make difficult decisions.

2. Good memory

Magicians need to remember rituals, ingredients lists, and spells.

3. Creative

Magicians need to adapt existing spells and rituals to new situations.

4. Self-disciplined and focused

A magician needs to be able to concentrate and shut out distractions, even under difficult circumstances. A good magician possesses enormous self-control and is able to resist temptations. She is probably the kind of person who can stick with a diet, and never goofs off to play computer games until the current job is done.

5. Patient

The study of magic requires endless practice and repeats, most of them boring, so impatient people drop out of the training before they achieve much. A good magician can spend hours sitting still, watching a candle flame or listening to the sound of the wind in the trees, if that's what the spell requires.

6. Highly trained

Mere talent is not enough.

Magic requires intense, prolonged study and practice. If she's a powerful magician, she has probably studied magic for many years. More about this in Chapter 3.

7. Specialist

She is probably highly skilled in one particular area such as improving livestock, changing the weather, building wealth, protection, or healing.

Think of magic as the equivalent of medicine. Just as there are dentists, chiropodists, aromatherapists, psychiatrists, Reiki healers and brain surgeons, magicians specialise.

8. Musical

Many forms of magic involve drumming or chanting; it helps if she has an ear for tunes and a strong sense of rhythm. However, this is not always necessary.

9. Spiritual

Most forms of magic are linked with religious practice. Your magician may be devoutly religious and begin every ritual with a prayer. Even if she's an atheist, she probably engages in spiritual practices such as meditation.

10. Studious

Magicians are always keen to learn more - expanding their own skills range, acquiring new spells, understanding other forms of magic, exploring natural and philosophical subjects.

Whenever she can, she seeks instruction in some subject or other. Many magicians amass vast collections of books, or sign up for every available online class. Your magician can often be found with her head in a book, and if your story is set in a pre-literate period, she listens avidly to bards and storytellers.

11. Well-organised and methodical

The best magicians always have information and ingredients at hand and know where to find them, and they have their equipment assembled before they begin the ritual. They keep careful records of the ingredients and exact wording used in every spell, and they measure the results. A disorganised, scatter-brained magician will probably not make it to the top of her profession.

12. Introvert

Most magicians like quietude and solitude.

Given the choice, your magician probably prefers spending time alone in nature over partying with noisy crowds. After a night in close company with many people, she needs a day alone in nature to recharge her energies. She may even be a loner.

However, some magicians are gregarious, sociable extroverts.

13. Ethical

Magic gives a person enormous power, and requires moral judgement to apply this power wisely and for the good.

All magicians have ethic codes of conduct, and they take them seriously. These may be based on their religion, the principles of their form of magic, the rules of their coven, or their individual conscience.

Modern magicians often follow the principles 'Harm none' and 'Don't interfere with someone's free will'. Some consider it wrong to accept money for magic. In other cultures and periods, other rules applied. If writing about a fantasy world, you can invent rules.

You can create powerful conflicts if your magician's goal conflicts with her ethics.

Perhaps the only way to help her child/rescue her lover/save the world is to do something against her conscience and against her magic's rules. Even the villain of your story, the evil sorcerer, abides by strict ethical rules.

You can have fun inventing them, for example 'Be kind to animals' (hurting humans is okay), 'Never harm a minor' (wait until they're eighteen), 'Never sacrifice a virgin girl' (deprive her of her virginity first).

14. Sharp senses

Your magician probably has keen eyesight and good ears, and her senses of smell, touch and taste are more refined than those of most people.

This natural ability has probably been refined over years of practice. Now she can recognise barks by how they feel in the hand, and identify crumbs of dried herbs by their smell. However, it is possible to work magic even with impaired senses. For example, your magician could be blind, as long as her other senses are well-developed.

15. Descended from magicians

Magical talent is often, though not always, genetically inherited. Perhaps her parents and siblings are also magicians, or perhaps her revered great-grandmother was a famous witch. You can compare this to how musical talent often runs in families. Think of the Mozart and Bach families, which produced extraordinary musicians and composers.

On the other hand, it is also plausible that your heroine is the only one in her family with a talent for magic.

16. Psychic

Although magical and psychic gifts are separate matters, many magicians have some psychic abilities as well.

They may, under certain circumstances, be able to read thoughts or see into the future. Avoid giving them too much talent, though. A character who excels at both magic and psychic gifts can solve too many problems too easily, which would make the story boring.

17. Day Job

Few magicians can make a living from their magic. Most have day-jobs. Surprisingly many modern magicians work in the medical sector: nurses, aromatherapists, doctors, complementary medicine practitioners, Reiki healers, massage therapists. Others are employed in scientific or engineering fields (using their analytical minds) or they work in the arts (using their creativity).

18. Pet

Magicians often have a close relationship with an animal. This can be a conventional pet, or an unusual animal. If the animal is involved in any way in the magician's work, it may be called a 'familiar'. A cat is a good choice for a familiar, because cats have highly developed paranormal senses. Readers like stories with animals, so giving your magician character a familiar can help boost your book's popularity.

All magicians are different. You can choose which of those traits suit your magician's character profile and your story's plot.

FOOD FOR THOUGHT

1. Think of a fictional magician in a novel you've read. Which of the traits does this person have?

2. Students on my *'Writing About Magic and Magicians'* course have commented that most of the attributes also describe a typical writer. Why do you think this is? In what ways are the work of an author and that of a magician similar?

ASSIGNMENT

Which of these seventeen traits apply to your magician character?

CHAPTER 2: MAGIC SYSTEMS

To make the magic in your novel plausible, use a system which already exists and works - or invent one which is based on an existing system.

PICK A SYSTEM

There are many different systems of magic, each with its own values and rules. Select one which suits your novel, and stick with it.

If you choose to invent a system, I recommend that you model it closely on an existing one, because this will make it plausible.

Here are some magic systems to choose from. The definitions are basic; just enough to help with your plot and to get you started on further research. The systems overlap; the magic your character practices may belong to more than one category. Many more systems exist, and each comes in several variations.

I'm also suggesting personality traits for characters practising some of those systems. Naturally, these aren't statements about what all wiccans and all shamans are like, just ideas for your fiction characters.

High Magic and Low Magic

This distinction exists mostly in the western world from the Middle Ages onwards. It doesn't imply that one is superior to the other. Mostly, it's about the level of education required.

High Magic requires the magician to study from books, and the ingredients are often expensive. This means he has to be literate, have the money to buy books, tools and ingredients, and have the leisure to read and carry out experiments.

In practice, this means that High Magic has been practised mostly by men of the upper classes.

The typical practitioner of High Magic is male, highly educated, and rich. He may use the word 'wizard' to describe his role. Example: a court wizard in the king's employ.

Among the lower classes, women, the peasantry, and people with limited funds and education, Low Magic has been more common. Since it's often taught orally, it doesn't require reading skills, and the basic ingredients such as water and herbs are available even to the poor.

The typical practitioner of Low Magic is female, networked with other women, with little education and little time for study, poor, and good at making do. Example: a medieval village witch.

In non-western cultures, this distinction often doesn't exist.

Black Magic and White Magic

'White' is supposed to be moral and good, and 'black' is supposed to be immoral and villainous. Most real magicians find this laughable. It's not the magic system which is good or bad, it's what the magician does with it (the means and the purpose).

However, clever magicians sometimes tell everyone that they're white magicians (white witches, white wizards, white shamans etc.), because it's reassuring for the neighbours. It also looks good on business cards.

Rebellious teenagers sometimes pride themselves in working 'Black Magic' - but many of those kids are just wannabes.

Ceremonial Magic

Ceremonial Magic involves a lot of ritual, recitation (sometimes in ancient languages such as Latin, Aramaic or Sanskrit), re-enactment, performance, special garments, and chanting. Often, though not always, it's religious (for example, practised by the priesthood of a temple). Most of the time, it's High Magic.

A well-known form is Enochian Magic.

The typical practitioner is male and educated. He possesses great confidence and a good memory.

Natural Magic

Natural Magic involves ingredients from nature, such as herbs and water. It may be practised outdoors, in a kitchen, or in a laboratory. The rituals are simple and short. The ingredients matter, and the magician studies nature and observes how the ingredients react. Natural Magic can be High Magic (for example, Alchemy) or Low Magic (for example, Folk Magic and Witchcraft).

The typical practitioner is observant, patient, blessed with good sight, hearing, taste and smell, and always aware of the phases of the moon.

Religious Magic

It's not the magician who works the magic, but a deity. The god works through the magician. The magician prays, and asks her god to work this miracle. It also helps if the client believes and joins the prayer.

Most religions have their form of magic - although some would not use the word 'magic'; they more common word is 'miracle'.

Each religion views the miracles of another religion with suspicion (and that's putting it mildly). Wiccan Witchcraft and Voodoo are largely religious magic.

Some Religious Magic is bound to specific items (e.g. relics of saints) or places (e.g. sites of pilgrimage). Sometimes, elements of Religious Magic creep into other magic systems, for example, a witch may use a sentence or a page from her religion's holy book to make a talisman. Religious Magic typically has a ceremonial element.

The purpose is often healing (i.e. faith healing); in some cultures, magic and medicine are intertwined. Sometimes, religious magicians are also psychics or dream interpreters.

The typical practitioner is spiritual and devout, and he may be deeply suspicious of other religions. He probably wears a pendant with the symbol of his religion, begins each ritual with a prayer or an invocation, and concludes it by thanking his patron deity.

Alchemy

If you're writing historical novels, Alchemy is an interesting system to choose. It was widely practised during the European Middle Ages and Renaissance, and also in the Islamic world and other cultures, with roots going back to Hellenistic Egypt and possibly even further.

Alchemy is both High Magic and Natural Magic, and may include spiritual, philosophical, mythological and religious concepts. Nowadays, few people practice Alchemy, and if they do, it's usually as an addition to their main system of magic.

The typical alchemist is male, educated, patient, and driven. He may be a 'mad scientist' type. He may come from a middle class background, but work (or aspire to work) among the upper classes.

The tools includes writing materials, astronomical charts, and the laboratory equipment of the period.

Traditional Witchcraft

Traditional Witchcraft is a form of Low Magic, and it may feature in historical novels.

In early historic periods, the witch played an important role in village life and was respected and sometimes feared. When witchcraft became outlawed, practitioners had to give up, work in secret, or risk torture and execution.

Little is known about Traditional Witchcraft in early European history. The witches themselves were illiterate and didn't write anything down. Their enemies wrote a lot, but with the purpose of maligning witchcraft, so they made up shocking things like child sacrifice and sex with the devil.

Traditional Witchcraft definitely doesn't involve devil worship, because it precedes Christianity, and the earlier Celtic religion didn't even have a devil.

Most witches practice on their own, because each village can support only one witch, and they seldom have the money or the means to travel to meet others.

Nowadays, Traditional Witchcraft is practised almost only in non-western cultures. In the west, it has become largely assimilated into Wiccan Witchcraft.

The typical practitioner is female, uneducated, illiterate, practical, resourceful and poor. She probably has a good memory and well-developed senses.

Tools used in Traditional Witchcraft were simple household implements - such as a cauldron, a broom, a knife - because the women were too poor to buy additional equipment and made do with what they already owned, and also because the use of basic household tools didn't arouse the inquisitors' suspicion.

Wiccan Witchcraft

If you write contemporary fiction, Wiccan Witchcraft is the system your character is most likely to use. This is modern witchcraft, based on the religion of Wicca. Since it is the most widely spread magic system in the western world, you'll find many excellent books and informative websites about it.

Although it draws inspiration from Traditional Witchcraft and borrows components from other religions and magic systems, Wiccan Witchcraft developed mostly in the second half of the twentieth century. Despite its relative youth, it's a powerful magic system, and has many practitioners. It is a form of Natural Magic as well as Religious Magic.

The Wiccan religion is based on nature worship and the polarity between female and male, and the magician often begins the ritual with an invocation to a goddess and a god, who are often called 'Lady' and 'Lord'. The Lady is frequently shown as having three aspects - Maiden, Mother and Crone - and the Lord may be depicted with horns (which can lead outsiders to the impression that witches worship the devil). Other deities may be worshipped as well.

Wiccan Witchcraft emphasises ethics; the magician must consider the implications of each spell carefully, and not use magic to cause harm. The focus of Wiccan Magic is often on healing.

Wiccan Magic is often practised out of doors, and some practitioners perform magic in the nude (which they call 'skyclad'). Wiccan Witchcraft uses the phases of the moon: spells for creating or increasing something work best during the waxing moon, while the waning moon is best for making something go away.

A spell concludes with the phrase "So mote it be." Witches meeting may greet one another with "Merry Meet." Group meetings are closed with "Merry Meet and Merry Part and Merry Meet Again." Letters are concluded with "Blessed Be."

Wiccans like to gather in groups called 'covens', or to meet once a month or for major festivals. A coven leader may be called the 'high priestess' or 'high priest'. However, there is no overall ruler of Wicca.

The major festivals are Beltane (1st May) and Samhain (1st November). These dates play a major role in Wiccan Witchcraft; so if your story occurs around one of those dates, make sure your character is doing something special.

The typical practitioner of Wiccan Witchcraft is a 'New Age' person (possibly a vegetarian tree-hugging pacifist type, who wears unbleached cotton, and shuns genetically modified food), more likely female than male, spiritual, religiously tolerant, open-minded, ethical, curious, able to think outside the box.

She practices Wiccan Witchcraft as a hobby rather than a career, and her day-job may be in a field of medicine or healing (she may be a nurse or an aromatherapist). She owns many books about Wicca, and also about other systems of magic as well as related subjects.

Typical Wiccan tools are a chalice, a knife (called 'athame'), a wand (a stick about a foot or two long), candles, herbs, crystals, and essential oils. Many Wiccan witches keep a 'Book of Shadows' (a combination or recipe book, spells collection, record of magic worked, and spiritual journal). Wiccans often wear a pendant with a five-pointed star, usually silver.

Necromancy

In this system, the magician summons a dead person, either as a ghost or spirit, or sometimes bodily. This is done to enlist the dead person's help, perhaps asking them for elusive information ("Where did you hide your will?"), advice ("How can we drive out the invading hordes?"), or assistance ("Join our army and drive out the invading hordes.")

The summoned person may be a long-dead ancestor, someone recently deceased, or a famous person of the past. Necromancy can be related to Shamanism, as well as to some forms of psychic work such as channelling and Spiritualist seances.

Necromancy lends itself to ghost stories, paranormal, historical and horror fiction. The Witch of Endor who summons the shade of Samuel in the Bible is a necromancer.

The typical practitioner is psychically gifted, strong-willed and courageous.

Shamanism

Shamanism is a Low Magic system. The shaman intercedes between the human world and the spirit world by communicating with spirits, and often by travelling into the spirit world to obtain information.

The focus of Shamanism is on healing the body, mind or spirit. Sometimes, the shaman may travel into the spirit world to retrieve the piece of the client's soul that has been missing. Such journeys can be dangerous and are not to be undertaken lightly.

The 'Change of Consciousness' phase of the ritual is important and extended in Shamanism. Shamans use drums (as well as chanting, dancing, drugs) to alter their consciousness.

Practising shamans usually work alone, but eventually choose a successor to train, usually a child (sometimes an adult), who shows certain indications (such as an affinity for drumming, or a tendency to climb trees). The chosen apprentice is supposed to accept the calling, even if it comes as a surprise.

Shamans can be found in most countries on most continents, although they are rare in Europe. Modern westerners often refer to native shamans in other cultures as 'witchdoctors'.

Shamanism is related to Necromancy, because both systems are based on communication with spirits, including the spirits of deceased people. However, the necromancer typically summons the spirits into the human world, while the shaman travels into the spirit world to meet them.

The typical shaman is musical, sensitive, with a strong sense of rhythm, psychic, courageous.

Tools and ingredients include drums, bells, a costume with feathers, herbs, bones, smoke and mind-altering drugs.

Ancient Egyptian Magic

For historical novelists, Ancient Egyptian Magic is an interesting system, because the Egyptians were regarded as the most powerful magicians in the ancient world.

Ancient Egyptian Magic is a form of Religious Magic, and it may overlap with religion, with medicine, and with psychic work.

The deities most frequently invoked are the goddess Selket (aka Serquet) for any magical purpose; the goddess Aset (aka Isis) for big or difficult magic and for raising the dead; and the god Thoth for anything to do with sickness and healing.

The emphasis of Ancient Egyptian Magic is on protection (for example against curses, murder or scorpion stings), and this is often done through an amulet or talisman.

The precise wording of a spell is important, and an error in the recitation can lead to disaster. The famous story of the sorcerer's apprentice who gets into trouble when he forgets the words for stopping the bathwater spell originates in ancient Egypt. Colours also play an important role. For magic to affect someone, the magician must know that person's true name.

The most important shape is the circle or oval which has protective qualities. Contrary to what most people think, the pyramid shape has no magical significance, although it has spiritual as well as practical purposes.

The typical practitioner is male, literate, much better educated than the average person, with an excellent memory. He is probably a priest attached to a temple, although he may be a secular magician with a side-line in medicine.

The tools are kept and carried in a box, much like a modern doctor might always carry a doctor's bag. The most important tool is a curved wand.

Folk Magic

This is a form of Low Magic, practised not by professionals but by amateurs.

It doesn't require much training, or expensive ingredients.

A peasant knows magic to make the barley ripen before the rain, a housekeeper uses a spell to keep rats out of the pantry, and a teenage girl uses a ritual to reveal the face of her future husband.

Typically, these people know just a handful of spells, and pass them on to members of their family or tribe.

Folk Magic is closely related to Traditional Witchcraft.

Voodoo

Voodoo is Religious Magic (based on African religions and Catholic Christianity), and Low Magic (using largely oral traditions rather than written works).

The rituals are usually held in private, and may involve communication with spirits, especially the spirits of ancestors and saints. Voodoo is commonly used to cure ailments, confound enemies, and obtain desires.

Tools and ingredients include herbs, stones, oils, bones and dolls. The dolls may be used to either harm or bless; contrary to common perception, Voodoo practitioners don't usually stick needles into dolls to cause harm.

INVENT A SYSTEM

In paranormal and fantasy fiction, you can invent a system of magic.

To keep it plausible, I recommend choosing an existing system, and using your imagination to adapt it.

You can also mix and match components from two or more systems to create your own.

By basing your invented system on real systems, you know that it works (at least hypothetically), and the reader will sense the authenticity.

TERMS, DEFINITIONS, SPELLINGS

<u>Choosing the right words</u>

If your character is clearly a shaman, a necromancer, or a witch, use that term. Otherwise, the word 'magician' is always appropriate, and if that's too long, you can use the short form 'mage'.

However, I advise against 'magus' (plural 'magi') which properly belongs to practitioners of the ancient Zoroastrian faith who practised magic, astronomy and alchemy. The wise men who come to Bethlehem in the Bible story are magi.

'Witch' is not a female wizard, and 'wizard' is not a male witch. Witches and wizards are practitioners of two very different magic systems.

The word 'warlock' is also contentious. It really means 'oath-breaker' or 'traitor', and doesn't describe a magician. Your readers may find it offensive, and reject your novel because of its use. However, since the word is often used (or misused) to mean 'male witch', especially in Scotland, you could have non-magical characters talk about a 'warlock', thus revealing their ignorance.

'Witchdoctor' is another word used by ignorant outsiders, usually by westerners for the shamans, faith healers, witches and folk magicians of other cultures.

The word 'sorcerer' is also used by outsiders, rather than by the magicians themselves, and it implies that the person is dangerous or evil.

A group of magicians is sometimes called a 'coven', though this applies mostly to Wicca and Traditional Witchcraft. A magician who works on her own is called a 'solitary'.

A 'conjurer' is not a genuine magician, but someone who can create effects which impress an audience. Conjurers use sleight of hand, double-bottomed containers, the colour black, mirrors, thumb-tips (plastic finger skins worn over the real finger), thin slippery silk scarves, optical illusions and misdirection. They entertain at cabaret shows, children's parties and so on.

The modern word for a professional who entertains audiences with conjuring is 'illusionist'. Some genuine magicians do conjuring to spice up their real magic for onlookers.

Magic vs Magick

Normally, 'magic' is the correct spelling.

However, 'magick' is also used, especially by insiders who wish to emphasise that they mean the real thing, not conjuring. You'll find this spelling mostly in a New Age and Wiccan context. You may also find 'majik' and other fancy spellings.

Capitalised or not?

The magic systems are sometimes capitalised, sometimes not, and the rules are not firm. When the term involves a religion or nationality, it's almost always capitalised (e.g. Wiccan, Catholic, Egyptian). Other words are capitalised in some books, but not in others (e.g. High Magic or high magic).

You can choose - just be consistent in your book. In this book, I'm capitalising the names of all magic systems, whether they are religious or not.

BLUNDERS TO AVOID

* Using 'witch' as the female of 'wizard', and 'wizard' as the male of 'witch'... as if these were gender distinctions.

* Calling modern magicians 'magi' ... as if they were Zoroastrians.

* Writing about a 'King of Witches' or 'Queen of Witches' ... as if witchcraft were a monarchy.

* Applying the principles of Wiccan Witchcraft to Traditional Witchcraft ... as if medieval witches were followers of the New Age.

* Assuming that the rules and rituals of one magic system apply to all kinds of magic ... as if ancient Egyptians practised New Age Wicca.

* Witches worshipping the devil... as if they believed in him.

FURTHER READING

Ancient Egyptian Magic by Bob Brier

Liber Null & Psychonaut: An Introduction to Chaos Magic by Peter J. Carroll

Italian Witchcraft: The Old Religion of Southern Europe by Raven Grimassi

Book of Shadows: A Modern Woman's Journey Into the wisdom of witchcraft by Phyllis Curott

What Witches Do by Stewart Farrar

Hedge Witch: A Guide to Solitary Witchcraft by Rae Beth

Witchcraft: A Beginner's Guide by Teresa Morey

Ancient Christian Magic by Marvin W. Meyer and Richard Smith

Spiritual and Demonic Magic: From Ficino to Campanella by D. P. Walker

Magic of the Celtic Otherworld: Irish History, Lore & Rituals by Stephen Blamires

Forbidden Rites: A Necromancer's Manual of the Fifteenth Century by Richard Kieckhefer

Communing with the Spirits: The Magical Practice of Necromancy by Martin Coleman

Greek and Roman Necromancy by Daniel Ogden

Great Book of Magical Art, Hindu Magic and East Indian Occultism & The Book of Secret Hindu, Ceremonial, and Talismanic Magic by L. W. de Laurence

Northern Magic: Rune Mysteries and Shamanism by Edred Thorsson

Sympathetic Magic Of The Ainu - The Native People Of Japan by John Batchelor

Gypsy Magic: A Romany Book of Spells, Charms, and Fortune-Telling by Patrinella Cooper

The Druid Magic Handbook: Ritual Magic Rooted in the Living Earth by John Michael Greer and David Spangler

The Voodoo Hoodoo Spellbook by Denise Alvarado and Doktor Snake

The Keys to the Gateway of Magic: Summoning the Solomonic Archangels and Demon Princes (a 17th century book, edited by Stephen Skinner and David Rankine)

Nocturnicon by Konstantinos

Enochian Vision Magick by Lon Duquette

Simplified Qabala Magic by Ted Andrews

Fire in the Head: Shamanism and the Celtic Spirit by Tom Cowan

Of Water and the Spirit: Ritual, Magic and Initiation in the Life of an African Shaman by Malidoma Patrice Some

Ceremonial Magic: A Guide to the Mechanisms of Ritual by Israel Regardie

Magic and Alchemy by Rosemary Ellen Guiley

The 21 Lessons of Merlyn A study in Druid Magic and Lore by Douglas Monroe

Scottish Witchcraft: The History and Magick of the Picts by Raymond Buckland

Ancient Jewish Magic: A History by Gideon Bohak

Santeria: African Magic in Latin America by Migene Gonzalez-Wippler

The Complete Idiot's Guide to Alchemy by Dennis William Hauck

High Magic: Theory & Practice by Frater U.:D.:

Condensed Chaos: An Introduction to Chaos Magic by Phil Hine

FOOD FOR THOUGHT

Consider a novel you've read. What is the underlying magic system?

ASSIGNMENT

1. Into which - if any - of these systems does the magic of your novel fit? If you're inventing a system, which of these does it most closely resemble?

2. Browse the web for sites with information about the magic system you're using in your novel. What inspiration or ideas can you glean from them? Do they agree in all matters, or do they contradict each other in some aspects?

CHAPTER 3: TRAINING AND INITIATION

To become a mighty mage, your character needs training. Mere talent isn't enough.

Like in any other field, success in magic comes from a combination of natural gift, determination, study, and practice. It's similar to writing: you can have the greatest natural literary gift in the world, but unless you learn the craft and actually practice writing, you won't achieve your potential.

Give your magician character a backstory which includes training, or send him to magical school.

A human who possesses great natural talent but has not had proper training may make devastating mistakes. He may also be in great danger, because if he has not learnt to control his powers, supernatural forces and evil spirits will try to gain control over them.

TRAINING OPPORTUNITIES

1. School of Magic

Your novel may have a school of magic for children, a college of magic, a mage academy, or even a university offering postgraduate degrees in comparative magic and magical anthropology.

Students sign up for full-time study, most likely on tuition-bed-and-board basis. If the novel is set in the modern western world, the classes may meet the requirements of the national curriculum in addition to providing magical training. In ancient Egypt, most magicians were priests, and magician-priests were brought up from a young age at the temple.

Depending on the type of school and level of education, a magic school is likely to teach subjects of relevance to magicians: for example sciences (especially botany and chemistry), medicine (conventional, alternative or complementary), music (especially chanting and drumming), physical education (especially dancing), philosophy and ethics (especially the ethics of magic spells), ancient languages (e.g. Latin, Aramaic, Sanskrit), religion (especially if it's a temple school), astronomy, astrology, mythology, psychology, divination, and more. A modern school may also have compulsory classes in health and safety.

2. Apprenticeship

A master magician takes one or several apprentices. The apprenticeship is similar to that of other trades, bound by similar rules. Typically, the master signs a contract with the youngster's parent, which indentures the apprentice for several years, and in return, the master teaches his craft. There may be payment involved; either the parent paying the master or the master paying the apprentice.

The apprentices may live in the master's house, and practice under his instruction. Typically, they may be put to hard work, including non-magical chores such as scrubbing floors.

This form of magical training has been prevalent in many cultures and periods, especially for shamans.

3. Self-study

A magician can plausibly teach herself, learning from observation, trial and error. This suits reclusive, organised, studious types who have a high education, a lot of self-discipline and intense curiosity. She needs access to learning materials, as well as the money and leisure to devote herself to the study.

Self-taught magicians are plausible among the educated wealthy upper classes in the western world from the Renaissance onwards.

Sometimes, a magician has initially served an apprenticeship and outgrown her master (or fallen out with him), and is pursuing further studies on her own.

4. Part-Time Study

Although it takes several years of full-time training to become a professional magician, it's also possible to practice magic as a hobby, and to devote only a few hours every week to training.

The part-time path is particularly plausible in the modern world, where many adults take up magic while earning their bread from a day-job. Many organisations offer part-time classes: community colleges, Pagan religious groups, New Age societies.

Classes may be in classroom environments, by correspondence, or online. In about a year, the student can achieve enough skill to work a little magic, and this may be all a hobbyist wants. If she wishes to go further, then decades of part-time study can make her a magician of significant power.

5. Informal Learning

Non-professional magicians may pass on their skills informally, especially among family members. For example, a mother may teach her daughter a few things she picked up from her own mother, and make the little girl practice it until she gets it right.

The range of applications is limited, typically involving skills of practical everyday use, such as how to make the cow give more milk and how to make the potatoes boil faster.

This type of magic is often called 'Folk Magic'. It won't equip the student to battle the sorcerous evil overlord and save the world.

CANDIDATE SELECTION

Schools, universities and masters are choosy about the students and apprentices they take.

Before a candidate is accepted for training, there will be an interview and an aptitude test.

When testing future apprentices, magicians may check for one or all of the following:

- ability to concentrate

- ability to follow instructions

- creativity and imagination

- ability to visualise

- ability to memorise

- motivation (Why does this person want to learn magic? A candidate who replies "To hurt my enemies," "To get rich quick," "To seduce chicks," or "It sounds fun, much better than doing real work," will be rejected)

- moral integrity

- obedience (especially in traditional-style indentured apprenticeships)

- ability to control thoughts

- ability think and act under pressure

- patience

- health

- sensory awareness

- certain features traditionally attributed to magicians of that form of magic (e.g. Nepalese shamans may look for a child who instinctively climbs trees)

- natural affinity for magic

- existing skills in related fields (e.g. clairvoyance, astrology)

- faith and piety (especially for religious magic, e.g. training in temple schools)

In addition to the candidate's character and aptitude, other factors may play a role, such as money, politics and connections. A college may give preference to the offspring of distinguished alumni, and a master may take on the apprentice whose parents pay most.

THE DAILY GRIND OF LEARNING

Magic requires a lot of practice, which students may find tedious. Every spell needs to be drilled and repeated, perhaps hundreds of times. There'll be a lot of visualising exercises, sitting still for an hour while keeping an imagined image of a yellow brick or a red flame in the mind's eye. Some forms of magic involve a lot of rote learning and recitations, others require the steady stirring of simmering potions at just the right rhythm all night long. The average teenager will probably hate much of it.

EXAMPLES FROM LITERATURE

Harry Potter by JK Rowling. The children attend a specialist school, Hogwarts, for several years, studying several forms of magic and related subjects. The students at Hogwarts learn theory, but they also practice a lot, and some scenes show them practising until they get it right.

Mage Heart by Jane Routley. A historical fantasy novel, a story about a young girl who grows into her powers as a magician at the same time as she grows into womanhood. The heroine started her magical training as apprentice to her adoptive father, a magician. Then she enrolled in a College of Magic for several years of formal classes. The novel is set during her final year at college when she takes on a magic job to boost her finances.

Krabat by Otfried Preussler. A powerful YA dark fantasy novel, huge bestseller in Germany, winner of several literature prizes. It's little known in the English-speaking world, although it has been translated and published variously as *Krabat* and as *The Satanic Mill*. A boy starts an apprenticeship as a miller, and is delighted to discover that he'll learn magic at the same time. The dual apprenticeship - miller and magician - takes several years. Several apprentices and journeymen work at the mill. Gradually, the boy realises that the magic he delights in is evil.

With A Single Spell by Lawrence Watt-Evans. An enjoyable, light-hearted, humorous heroic fantasy. It plays with the idea 'What happens if an apprenticeship doesn't work out?' An apprentice magician is left stranded when his master dies. The master had used the apprentice for mundane tasks, always promising to teach him real magic, but never teaching any. The boy is too old to apprentice himself to a new trade, and he can't find another master willing to take him on. The only spell he knows is how to start a fire. Now he must make his way in the world with no other skill but arson.

The Amulet of Samarkand by Jonathan Stroud. A beautifully written, witty YA fantasy, highly enjoyable for adults as well. The government controls use of magic and arranges for talented children to be adopted by professional, government-approved magicians. An unusually talented precocious boy gets apprenticed to a not-very-good magician. While pretending to learn at the slow pace set by his master, he secretly teaches himself more advanced stuff, soon overreaching himself by the summoning a powerful demon. This is a combination of 'apprenticeship' and 'self-study'.

INITIATION

When the student has passed a probationary period, he is initiated into the craft.

This ritual often takes place during a solstice or equinox, or on an important festival of the religion (e.g. Beltane or Samhain for Wiccan Witchcraft). The student commits himself to the course of study, or even to a lifetime of service to the religion. As part of the ritual, he may change into a new robe of a different colour.

When the student completes his training, there may be a further initiation.

Some systems of magic have several levels of initiations called 'degrees'. As the student progresses, he achieves another degree, and is initiated into the next level. At each initiation, he may receive a differently coloured rope for tying his robe.

If several students are initiated at the same event, there may be a party or feast afterwards.

BLUNDERS TO AVOID

* The protagonist discovers that she has magical talent, and this makes her a powerful magician... as if magic didn't require study. That's the equivalent of getting a black belt in karate without any training, purely on the basis of natural talent.

* The protagonist discovers an ancient book of magical which instantly enables him to work spells... as if magic didn't require practice. That's the equivalent of someone finding a book on Russian grammar and instantly speaking fluent Russian.

* A master mage or an old witch invites a child to spend an afternoon with her, and in this time she teaches the kid everything she knows... as if a lifetime of learning could be crammed into a few hours. That's the equivalent of becoming a brain surgeon by spending an afternoon with a brain surgeon.

* On entering the magic academy, the student is immediately initiated without probationary period.

* Without probationary period or proper information, an aspiring magician commits himself for the rest of his life.

FOOD FOR THOUGHT

1. Have you read a work of fiction about a magician in training? How plausible do you find it?

2. Have you read a story (or seen a movie) involving a magic initiation ritual? Looking back, how realistic was it?

ASSIGNMENT

1. Take notes about the training your magician is undertaking, or has undertaken: how long is the training period? Who is teaching him? What skills and subjects does he study? Which aspects of his tuition does he like, and which does he hate?

2. If your magician is currently at school or in an apprenticeship, write a paragraph showing a typical learning situation.

3. If your magician has finished his training, write a paragraph in which he remembers something his instructor taught him, including the circumstances which made that lesson memorable.

CHAPTER 4: RITUAL AND POWER-RAISING

Each act of magic requires a ritual. Although the details depend on the system, the magician's preferences and level of skill, as well as the situation, the following is typical:

STRUCTURE OF THE RITUAL

1. Preparation

The magician reads the instructions, locks the door, dons her robe, gets her tools ready, assembles the ingredients and so on.

2. Casting the Circle

The magician creates a circle, either physically (e.g. by drawing it with chalk on the ground) or mentally (by visualising a circle around her). The circle serves to contain the power she raises, and also to protect her from harm. Dangerous spirits may be drawn by magic ritual, and the magician may be vulnerable to attack. The circle keeps her safe. (More about this in Chapter 5)

3. Invocation

The magician calls on assistance from the spirit world. This may be a prayer to her god or goddess, with a request that they lend a helping hand, an invitation to ancestral spirits to join her, or a summoning of a demon. In Religious Magic, this may be a prayer, or a long and complex rite. In other systems, it may be short or even left out. In High Magic, the spirits are usually 'summoned'; in Wiccan Witchcraft, they are 'invoked' and 'invited'. Sometimes, this phase also includes an offering to the gods or spirits, for example, a libation of wine or milk poured at the base of a tree, or - in the case of darker magic - a bowl of blood to welcome the demon.

You can deal with the invocation part in just a few words, for example, >After a brief prayer to Hecate, she...< or >he cast the circle, invoked the spirit of Saint Whatshisname, and...<

4. Altering the State of Consciousness

The magician changes how her brain functions, to make it receptive to magic. Often, this involves going into a trance. Chanting, dancing or drumming work well for this. Some magicians use deep meditation, others take mind-altering drugs as a short-cut.

5. Raising Power

Magic needs energy, and the magician taps into an energy source or creates energy. This is an important phase of the ritual; without it, magic will not work. More about this later in this chapter.

6. Speaking the Spell

The magician speaks or chants the words of the spell. In some magic systems (such as Ancient Egyptian Magic), it's essential to get the words, pronunciations and intonations exactly right. In others (such as Wiccan Witchcraft) the words are merely a vehicle by which the spell travels, and what matters is the intent, i.e. the magician needs to concentrate fully on the purpose of the spell.

More about this in Chapter 7.

In Shamanism, this is the stage during which the shaman travels to the spirit world, and in Necromancy, this is when the necromancer asks questions of the deceased person.

7. Dismissing the Spirits

Once the spell is cast, the magician thanks the spirits for their assistance (if she invited them) or dismisses them (if she summoned them), or says another prayer to her goddess or god.

8. Closing the circle

The magician dismantles the physical circle, or visualises the imaginary circle as fading.

9. Grounding

The magician needs to come back to reality, especially if the ritual involved journeying to the spirit world. The quickest and easiest is to drink some water and eat a little bread.

10. Keeping Records

Like a scientist conducting experiments, the magician records what exactly she did during the ritual, with which ingredients, what the purpose was, how it felt, and so on. This allows her to keep track of the efficacy of the magic, and learn for future rituals. An alchemist's record-keeping is probably factual and analytical, while a Wiccan witch's entry into her Book of Shadows is more about emotions and perceptions.

11. Resting

Magic is mentally, emotionally and physically exhausting. After working major magic, your character needs a rest. If the plot permits, allow her a nap. If you're a devious writer, you can make things difficult for her, and let her worst enemy attack just at this moment when she's weak and vulnerable.

Stages 2, 3, 4 and 5 are sometimes carried out in a different order or combined. For example, by drumming and dancing, the shaman can change her consciousness and raise power at the same time.

The ritual can take as little as two seconds or as long as two days. A public ritual is likely to take longer than a private one, because the magician wants to please the audience.

An experienced magician may use a shorter ritual than an inexperienced one. Ritual helps the magic, and a novice needs all the help she can get. An inexperienced magician gets best results if she adheres to the ritual precisely and takes a lot of time. A veteran mage can do something in minutes or seconds because she has the experience. That's as with other things: knitting your first pair of socks is going to take a long time, but by the time you've completed your hundredth pair, you can produce them really fast.

FICTION IDEAS FOR POWER-RAISING

All magicians raise power somehow. If the term 'power-raising' sounds too much 'New Age' for your historical novel, you can invent a different phrase.

The magician can raise power in many different ways, and she may use more than one source.

* She may draw the energy from within herself, by taking actions which create energy (dancing and drumming are especially effective). Her own intense emotions can add extra fuel.

* She may tap into the existing magical energies of the environment, for example stone circles, ley lines, ancient monuments, sacred sites, running water, sunlight or fire. (More about this in Chapter 5)

* She may use the magical energy contained in objects, for example crystals (especially in Wiccan Witchcraft) or relics (especially in Religious Magic).

* She can ask gods or spirits to lend power to her magic, especially if she practices Religious Magic.

* She may draw on energy from other people. For example, if the whole village gathers to help a magician call rain, then those people's enthusiasm can be harnessed. An evil magician may draw her energy from her victims' pain and fear.

A magician may use more than one source of power. For example, a Wiccan may pray to the Lady and the Lord, invoke the spirits of the winds, perform the ritual on the intersection of two ley lines, use a charged amethyst crystal, and dance herself into a trance.

The magician feels the power inside her body as well as around her.

Some magicians perceive it as a surge of energy pulsing through the blood, others as a heat storm around them. Some say it feels like the whole body being stung with nettles inside and out, yet others liken it to waltzing while tipsy on champagne.

Wiccan witches describe the power as rising out of their head and spiralling upwards in a cone shape. You can use your imagination, as long as your magician feels something.

BLUNDERS TO AVOID

* The magician simply points a wand and speaks a few words and magic happens... as if magic didn't require power.

* The magician summons a god or goddess... as if deities would obey human commands.

* A religious magician doesn't pray at the beginning and end of the ritual... as if her power didn't come from the divine.

FOOD FOR THOUGHT

Have you read a work of fiction in which a character worked magic? Which of the stages are recognisable?

ASSIGNMENT

1. For a magic scene in your novel, plot out the structure of the ritual. What does your magician do at each stage? Feel free to combine or leave out some stages to make it appropriate to your story.

2. Write a draft paragraph for your work in progress: a few sentences in which your magician raises power. What does she do, and how does it feel?

CHAPTER 5: LOCATION AND CIRCLE-CASTING

This chapter will be useful for most of you, regardless of what kind of magic you're writing about.

Most magicians can work magic in most places - but the location can make magic easier or more powerful.

CHOOSING THE VENUE

Magic works better in some places than in others, and each magician has a different preference.

Some magicians like to be near a stream, others under a tree, on a ley line (invisible energy line running in the earth or the air), or in a room with a north-facing window. Wealthy magicians, especially those practising High Magic, may have a whole room set aside for magic, called a 'temple', with purpose-designed interior and full equipment. Most alchemists have a laboratory. Many Wiccan witches prefer to work outside in nature.

With each use, the place gains more magical energy, so magicians like using the same place again and again. Venues used by generations of magicians are best. Stone circles positively hum with magical energy. For religious magic, the religion's sacred sites are best.

Some places are unfavourable for magic, for example, those which lack privacy. The proximity of electric power lines can also interfere with magic. However, at a pinch, a good magician can work magic anywhere.

HOW TO CAST THE CIRCLE

Almost all magicians of all traditions perform magic inside a circle, (though sometimes it's an oval). This circle holds in the magical power and keeps out harmful influences.

Where possible, the magician uses a ready-made circle, for example, a circular grove of trees, an ancient stone circle, or a circle-shaped floor mosaic. Some magicians have circular rugs – often embroidered with mystical symbols – which they roll up after use and hide under the bed. A magician may draw a line in the sand or in the snow, or use charcoal or chalk to draw on the floor, or stick twigs or icicles into the ground to create a circle. Circles which can be wiped out after use are good for magicians who have to work in secret.

The magician can also create a circle in her mind, by visualising a ring of light or fire. Wiccan witches often use a ring of blue or white light.

The advantage is that this can be done anywhere (in a dungeon, in a crowd, on Mars) secretly, leaving no trace. However, this is very, very difficult, and requires much practice.

You may want to try it for yourself: Imagine yourself surrounded by a circle of blue light. How long can you hold the image in your mind? Perhaps for a second or two. The magician needs to hold it for several minutes, and at the same time focus on the power-raising, and on the purpose and targeting of the spell. Only a highly trained magician can do that.

Students of magic often don't have the patience to do the 'boring' visualisation exercises their teacher demands of them, and can't cast a strong mental circle when they need one.

A mental circle is easier to maintain if it's combined with a physical one, even if that physical one is far from perfect. A magician who needs to cast an emergency spell may look for something vaguely round – say, a pattern in a carpet, or an oil spill on the road – and build a mental circle on that.

When creating the circle, whether it's a physical or a mental one, the magician does it clockwise – at least in most parts of Europe (in some Asian and Middle Eastern traditions, the circle is cast anti-clockwise).

This is especially the case in Celtic societies where the direction has always been considered important, and the clockwise direction is believed auspicious. If your story is set in Scotland, you can be sure that your magician casts the circle clockwise.

In a historical novel, the word 'sun-wise' may be more appropriate than 'clock-wise'. If your story is set in Scotland, you can use the Gaelic word 'deiseal'. Wiccans spell it 'deosil'.

If several people participate in a magic ritual, they all need to be inside the circle before the ritual starts. At a large gathering, the people themselves form a circle with their bodies. The leading magician works in the centre of this circle.

CHOOSING THE TIME

Certain kinds of magic work best at certain times. The waxing moon is good for spells involving growth, the waning moon for banishment. However, this is not a definitive rule, since the moon phases affect different magicians differently. Some magicians, especially those practising High Magic, consult astronomical or astrological charts for auspicious dates, i.e. they may wait until a certain constellation reaches a certain place in the sky. In many traditions, the solstices and equinoxes are considered good dates for all kinds of magic.

The time of the day can also play a role. Some magicians say that healing magic works best in the morning, and wealth spells around noon.

In Celtic traditions, the season of the year is important. Magicians may schedule important spells to coincide with, say, the first hawthorn blossoms, the barley harvest or the first frost. In Wiccan Witchcraft, as well as Druidry and most Celtic traditions, the most favourable times of the year are around Beltane (1st May, good for fertility, growth and love spells) or Samhain (1st November, good for manifestations, psychic work and communicating with spirits).

PLOT POSSIBILITIES

Here are some ideas for spicing up the magic with conflicts and complications:

* What if it's an emergency, and the magician can't use her accustomed physical circle? What if the situation is so dangerous and dire that she can't concentrate enough to create a mental circle and hold it in her mind?

* What if the student magician who skipped her visualisation exercises desperately needs to create a mental circle, and can't do it?

* What if the magician casts a mental circle, but it's an insufficient one, and demons enter the circle and hijack her magic?

* What if the magician needs to perform an urgent spell, and it's the wrong phase of the moon?

FOOD FOR THOUGHT

Have you read a work of fiction in which the magician has a special place for working magic? How does she cast the circle?

ASSIGNMENT

1. Decide how and where your magician casts her circle. Does she have a regular venue? Is she ever forced to work magic in a different place? If so, what does she do?

2. Write a short section for your work in progress, showing how and where your magician character casts the circle. This may be just a sentence or two (if all goes to plan) or several paragraphs (if the plot throws challenges at the magician).

CHAPTER 6: COSTUMING AND EQUIPMENT

In this chapter, we'll dress and equip your magician. Although special garments and tools aren't always necessary, they're helpful.

WHAT THE MAGICIAN WEARS

Most magicians have a special garment for performing magic, something which makes them feel special and gives them confidence.

For Religious Magic, the practitioner may wear beautiful clothes to honour their deity.

When performing for an audience (a paying client, or a religious congregation), stunning clothes can impress.

Often, the garment is a robe, a long garment. The colour may be significant. Some magicians wear either black or white, because these are neutral colours. Others prefer a bold colour such as purple, red or royal blue. In some hierarchical organisations, magicians wear robes according to their ranking or degree. Sometimes, the robe remains the same colour, but the rope tying it around the waist changes in colour as the candidate advances through the degrees.

When magicians wish to stay unobserved - for example, if magic is illegal and a group of them perform magic outdoors - they prefer black, because this makes them almost invisible, especially at night.

In some branches of Wiccan Witchcraft, practitioners perform magic in the nude, because they aim to be close to nature. Since they also aim to do it out of doors, they need a private location, or they may get unwelcome attention from voyeurs and passers-by. Wiccans use the poetic word 'skyclad' for outdoors nudity.

Jewellery is often silver, and almost always contains gemstones (especially for High Magic) or crystals (especially for Wiccan Witchcraft).

Since hair can conduct magic, most magicians wear their hair loose during the ritual.

EQUIPMENT

Here's a list of items which your fictional magician may use:

* Most magicians use a stick. It's called 'wand' if it's shorter than an arm, and 'staff' if it's longer. It may be plain or decorated. Sometimes it contains a crystal. Usually it is straight, though ancient Egyptian magicians used curved sticks. Some magic traditions specify that it must be naturally fallen wood, not cut from a living tree. The wand or staff is used to direct magic, like an extension of the arm.

* A knife. In many western systems, including Wiccan Witchcraft, this is called 'athame'. It may be blunt for mere ritual use, or it may be sharp and used for practical purposes such as chopping herbs and cutting threads. It often has a black handle.

* Symbols of the elements. Different magical traditions have different elements. For example, Wicca uses Earth, Air, Fire and Water (sometimes with Ether as a fifth element). Chinese magic uses Earth, Fire, Wood, Water, Metal. Ancient Mesopotamian magic used Salt Water and Fresh Water. Water may be symbolised by a bowl of water, Fire by a candle. In some traditions, the knife symbolises Fire (in others, it symbolises Air), and the wand symbolises Air (in others, it symbolises Fire).

* Crystals can increase the power of magic. They're like batteries, storing and releasing energy. Rose quartz is especially good for love spells and relationships, citrine for business and money matters, and amethyst for spiritual and psychic quests.

* An image or symbol of the deity the magician worships, for example, a statue of a goddess. Some magicians pick and mix statues from several religions. If the magician has her own temple, or works in a religious venue, there is probably a permanent altar. Other magicians may have small portable altars which they set up for the ritual, and dismantle afterwards.

* Materials and ingredients for making potions, amulets, talismans and such. These can include paper, scraps of coloured fabric, ribbons in symbolic colours, dried herbs, string, etc.

* A sacred/spiritual/magical journal, and writing implements. If the magician is literate, she writes up her experience after the ritual, to keep a record of what magic has been done when, and to study the effects. In Wiccan Witchcraft, this is called a 'Book of Shadows'.

* Candles, incense, matches or lighter. The colour of the candles is often significant, for example, pink for love spells, green for money magic. The incense may serve to help the magician change levels of consciousness, or to purify the place (e.g. in Shamanism, the practitioner may use smudging herbs).

* A spellbook (sometimes called 'grimoire'), or a written liturgy, spell or instructions. Written notes are useful, especially if the magician is working this kind of magic for the first time.

* Offerings for the gods or spirits, for example food, incense, perfume, wine, flowers.

* A musical instrument (probably a drum, rattle or bell), or a CD player with ambient music or chants. In Shamanism, this is usually a large tambourine; in Ancient Egyptian magic, it's a sistrum rattle.

* Anything else the magician (or her author) decides she needs.

PLOT POSSIBILITIES

* What if the magician needs to work magic, and she doesn't have access to her usual tools, or the necessary ingredients aren't at hand?

* What if the magician performs 'skyclad' and gets surprised in the act by someone who is either morally outraged by nudity, or tries to take advantage?

FURTHER READING

Cunningham's Encyclopaedia of Magical Herbs by Scott Cunningham

Cunningham's Encyclopaedia of Crystal, Gem & Metal Magic by Scott Cunningham

Practical Candle-burning Rituals: Spells and Rituals for Every Purpose by Raymond Buckland

Crystal Enchantments: A Complete Guide to Stones and Their Magical Properties by D.J. Conway and Brian Ed. Conway

Creating Magical Tools: The Magician's Craft by Chic Cicero and Sandra Tabatha Cicero

FOOD FOR THOUGHT

1. In a work of fiction you remember, what garments does the magician wear, and what tools does she use?

2. If you were a magician, what would you prefer: to use the same tools every time, or to improvise? Why?

ASSIGNMENT

1. What does your magician wear for magic?

2. What tools does she use regularly?

3. Write a sentence or paragraph in which the magician prepares to work magic.

CHAPTER 7: PHRASING THE SPELL

The word 'spell' can either refer to the act of magic, also called the 'ritual'. Or it can mean the words which are spoken, thought or chanted as the key part of the ritual.

In Ancient Egyptian Magic, and in some forms of High Magic, it's vital to pronounce the words correctly. Otherwise, disaster may ensue.

However, in most magic systems, what the magician thinks during the ritual is more important than the words he speaks. It's important to hold the intent in mind while speaking or chanting the words. The words are simply the vehicle that carries the magic. Getting a word wrong doesn't matter, but losing the concentration and thinking of something else can seriously mess up the magic.

It helps to learn the words by heart, or to have them written down, so that the magician can concentrate on the intent.

A magician can use an existing spell - perhaps one he has used before, one recommended by a magician friend, or one gleaned from a grimoire.

Alternatively, he can create his own spell for the purpose. Old spells are often more effective or easier to use; they hit the mark more neatly. It's as if the magic is travelling along a well-worn smooth road, instead of carving out a new path.

But new spells are good, too. Sometimes the magician wants to achieve something very specific for which no previous spell exists, or perhaps he doesn't like the existing spells.

Composing the words for a new spell is an enjoyable creative exercise, similar to writing poetry.

Readers enjoy seeing the words of a spell, so make one up, and have fun. Just don't use it as an excuse for forcing page-long poetry on your readers.

HOW TO WRITE A SPELL

Write the spell the way you would write a poem. Focus on making it sound good. The better it sounds, the easier it is to remember and recite, and the more smoothly it will travel. Use poetic techniques you like, for example:

* Meter. That's the rhythmic pattern. You can either use specific poetic meters, or simply put words together so they sound rhythmical.

* Repetition. Use the most important word several times.

* Alliteration. Several words in the spell start with the same sound.

* End-rhymes. The last words in the lines rhyme.

* Assonance. Several words contain the same vowel sound.

* Consonance. Several words contain the same consonants.

Most spells are very short - often between one and six lines - and the magician repeats them over and over.

Normally, the spells are in plain English (or plain whatever-language). However, High Magicians (who pride themselves on their superior education) like to use a dead language such as Latin, Hebrew or Sanskrit.

It's also possible to think the words of the spell, rather than say them aloud.

Some magic actions don't require any verbal spells at all.

SAMPLE SPELLS

Here are examples which use some of these poetic techniques:

"Waves and water, waves and water,
Bring me back my wayward daughter."

"Sacred spirits send me deep,
 soothing, restful, healing sleep."

"My wrath upon you for your wicked wrong!"

"Money flow, money come shower me.
Money grow, money empower me."

"Cower, computer! By my command, you shall crash no more!"

"Agent! Agent! Accept and adore this awesome author's beguiling book."

FURTHER READING

Composing Magic: How to Create Magical Spells, Rituals, Blessings, Chants, and Prayers by Elizabeth Barrette

FOOD FOR THOUGHT

1. Have you read a work of fiction in which the actual spell is quoted? Does the spell use any poetic techniques?

2. Newly-composed spells work. However, traditional much-used spells have more power. Why might this be so?

ASSIGNMENT

1. Just for fun, invent a spell for one of these:
* Losing weight
* Protecting house plants from greenfly infestation

* Motivating a couch potato go to the gym

* Keeping house keys from getting mislaid

2. Write a short spell for your magician character to use in the book.

CHAPTER 8: CORRESPONDENCES

Most Magic Systems use the energetic links between objects and concepts. Certain colours, herbs, gemstones, moon phases and seasons help certain kinds of magic.

These connections are called 'correspondences'. They allow the magician to invent a potent spell or create a talisman. For example, if a magician needs to quickly improvise a healing spell, she uses the colours, symbols, flowers, herbs, shapes, incenses etc. associated with healing magic.

USING CHARTS

While magicians memorise the important correspondences, they also use tables of correspondences as 'cheat sheets'.

You can find many similar charts online, especially on Wiccan websites (search for "Magic Correspondences"), and they seldom agree completely with one another.

That's because different Magic Systems use different correspondences. The connections also depend on the culture; for example, in Asia, colours have different meanings than in Europe. In addition, individual magicians may use correspondences which are personal to them.

Correspondences work through the magician's mind. Whatever that particular mage associates with that particular colour (perhaps because their instructor taught her, or because of a personal experience), that's what works best for that magician.

If you write about an existing Magic System, use the correspondences of that system. If you've invented a system, and especially if you've made up a fantasy world, you can invent correspondences.

You may want to create your own chart, based on what the colours and objects symbolise to you. That's how the colour correspondences mostly work: by what they mean to the magician. As the author, you're the magician who creates the fiction, so you're entitled to make up correspondences.

CORRESPONDENCE TOPICS

I suggest you include two to five of the following topics:

- Colours

- Crystals, minerals, gemstones (especially for Natural Magic and High Magic)

- Flowers, herbs, fruit, trees (especially for Natural Magic)

- Planets (especially for Alchemy)

- Constellations

- Moon phases (especially for Wiccan Witchcraft)
- Zodiac signs
- Incenses
- Chakras
- Deities or saints (especially for Religious Magic)
- Animals
- Mythological creatures
- Demons
- Angels (especially for Religious Magic)
- Body parts (especially for healing spells)
- Runes
- Tarot cards
- The four elements (Earth, Air, Fire, Water)
- Seasons of the year (especially for Natural Magic)
- Days of the week
- Chemical elements (especially for Alchemy)
- Geometric shapes
- Metals (especially for Alchemy)
- Numbers

You can also include anything else you like, but keep it simple.

LIST COLOUR CORRESPONDENCES

The most versatile of all correspondences is colour. Your fictional magician will almost certainly use colour correspondences., unless she's colour blind.

In modern magic, some major colour correspondences are these:

Red: passion, power, courage, willpower, fire, the Root chakra, sexual relationships, sexual potency, speed, strength, sports, energy, transformation

Orange: energy, joy, the Sacral chakra, sexuality, the abdomen, prosperity, celebrations, luck, fortune, business success, legal matters, ambition, personal creativity

Pink: romantic love, relationships, health, the Crown chakra, spirituality, bliss, nurturing, friendships, forgiveness, emotional healing, easing inner pain

Blue: spirituality, learning, the element Air, the element Water, the Throat chakra, truth, loyalty, serenity, tranquillity, sleep, creativity, poetry

Purple: psychic matters, clairvoyance, spiritual matters, justice, royalty, the Brow chakra, protection from negativity

Green: wealth, abundance, growth, healing, the element Water, the chest, the Heart chakra, fertility, rejuvenation, faerie

Turquoise: wealth, investments, the element Water, inventions, intellectual matters

Black: protection, neutralising harmful influences, the element Earth, calm

White: purity, the element Air, truth, enlightenment, new beginnings, clairvoyance, angels, forgiveness

Yellow: trade, communication, writing, knowledge, learning, the element Earth, the element Air, joy, mental clarity, concentration, alertness, travel, change, Solar Plexus chakra, telepathy, exams

Brown: the element Earth, crafts, buildings, home-making, common sense

Silver: wealth, spiritual matters, female

Gold: wealth, power, masculine, fame, overcoming addictions

Bronze: love, friendship, positive relationships, career success

Remember: you can change these to suit your story and your magician.

FURTHER READING

Llewellyn's Complete Book of Correspondences: A Comprehensive & Cross-Referenced Resource for Pagans & Wiccans by Sandra Kynes

FOOD FOR THOUGHT

To get into the mindset of a magician using correspondences, do this exercise: Imagine you're a mage whose ritual involves braiding coloured ribbons. Your client asks for a spell to bring them success.

What colours would you choose for the ribbons if your client is:

- a junior secretary seeking promotion to personal assistant?

- an inventor who wants to sell the patent for his invention?

- a wife who wants to rekindle the passion in her marriage?

- a shop owner who wants to revive her flagging business?

- a poet who wants help in overcoming writer's block?

- a law student who finds it difficult to concentrate to prepare for his final exams?

- a blogger who wants more subscribers?

- a romance writer seeking fame?

There are no right or wrong answers, and you can use personal associations as well as the correspondences listed above. Whatever you choose is right. Have fun.

ASSIGNMENT

Create a chart of magical correspondences for use in your fiction world.

CHAPTER 9: LOVE SPELLS

Love spells make great fiction, full of secrets, conflict, drama and passion.

Your character can cast her own love spell, or she can seek professional help from a witch, a ritual wizard, or other type of mage).

RITUALS

The most common ingredients used in the ritual are:

* roses (often red or pink)

* something from each of the two people (usually a lock of hair, and in modern times, a photograph)

* red or pink candles

* a fruit (for example, an apple)

* a crystal (rose quartz is a favourite)

* herbs (such as dittany or balm of Gilead)

* spices (especially cinnamon)

* red wine

* a ribbon (red or pink)

However, the ingredients vary between different types of magic, and individual magicians have their own preferences. The actual ritual also differs.

Here's a typical ritual for a love spell:

1. The magician may cut the fruit in halves, insert the locks of hair, and tie the fruit back together with the pink ribbon. Alternatively, she may brew a love potion which involves red wine simmering in a cauldron with rose petals, herbs and cinnamon.

2. If both people are present, the magician may link their hands and tie them with a ribbon or scarf.

If only one person is present, the spell won't be complete until the second person has become involved, for example, by drinking the love potion.

CLIENTS

Most clients are besotted with someone who doesn't reciprocate their feelings. They are convinced that this person is the one for them, that they're meant to be together, that they will not be fulfilled and happy until that person is theirs.

They also believe that the love spell is in the best interest of that person, and that the relationship will be a happy one if only the person would return their love.

They are desperate, can't bear the pain of their unrequited passion any longer, and are willing to pay almost any price for a love spell.

Other clients are lonely and looking for love.

They want a spell to help them find a mate. These include teenagers whose self-esteem is low because they don't have a boyfriend, single women whose biological clock is ticking, and men who can't get a date.

On rare occasions, a couple may seek a magician's help to save their crumbling marriage.

In historical fiction, parents and politicians may resort to love spells to bring about an advantageous match, or to bring affection to an arranged marriage.

Finally, the magician may resort to magic to win the person she desires for herself.

CONFLICTS

In some magic systems (especially modern ones), it's considered unethical to interfere with a person's free will. Although the magicians will happily help the couple who wish to strengthen their bond, and the lonely heart in search of a mate, they will refuse to force a specific person's feelings.

However, not all magicians have the same qualms. In earlier periods, magicians often made good money from love potions. Even today, many magicians advertise on the internet, promising to deliver one's heart's desire.

Some magicians compromise by creating spells which work only if there is already some affection between the couple. For example, the desired person must drink wine from the same cup as the client, immediately after he has drunk from it - something she wouldn't do if she hated him. An ancient Egyptian love spell required the man to anoint his member with a potion before having intercourse with the woman of his desire - and for that to happen, she already had to fancy him quite a bit.

Other magicians try to dissuade the client from focussing on a specific person. Instead, they recommend a general love spell, one which will help the client find a suitable mate.

DOES YOUR MAGICIAN PERFORM LOVE SPELLS?

What's your magician character's stance? Would she agree to interfere with the feelings of an unwilling person? Remember, most magicians have a strict code of ethics, so she has probably strong views on this.

A Wiccan witch would almost certainly decline, because her ethics don't allow interfering with a person's free will.

She would suggest a more generalised magic ritual, one which blesses the client with a happy relationship, but not with a specific person.

A Traditional witch, on the other hand, may not think twice about it. If she's a village witch in the Middle Ages, love potions may be a major source of income for her, and she depends on them for a living.

A High magician may turn up his nose at the request, because he doesn't stoop to such petty matters. He may make an exception if the king requests a ritual to bring about a dynastic marriage for his eldest son.

A shaman may decline because he doesn't know how to work love spells, and he may be surprised that the client thinks he can.

CONFLICT - PLOT POSSIBILITIES

For the strictly ethical magician, requests for love spells can lead to terrible dilemmas. Here are some ideas you may want to play with:

* What if the client is suffering terrible pain from unrequited love, and the magician wants to ease his suffering?

What if the desperate client is her own sister, her best friend, her son? What if turning down the request for a love spell causes a rift between them?

* What if the client won't take no for an answer? What if the client is the king, the chief inquisitor, or other powerful person? What if the client threatens to punish the magician for her refusal?

* What if the client is rich and willing to pay a lot for a love spell? What if the magician desperately needs money to save her lover or to feed her starving child?

* What if a ruthless magician agrees to waive his principles and grant the heroine the love spell she craves... but only if she pays a terrible price for it?

* What if the magician herself suffers from unrequited love? What if her ethics forbid her to manipulate someone's will, but she is convinced that it is for that person's own good? What if her need overrides her conscience?

CONSEQUENCES - PLOT POSSIBILITIES

Love spells interfering with someone's free will can lead to disaster. Here are some plot ideas:

* What if the love spell works at first, but wears off after the wedding? What if the person finds out that their spouse had trapped them with a love spell?

* What if the two people love each other, but their relationship is desperately unhappy - and they can't get out of it? What if they blame the magician for their misery?

* What if the client loses interest and wants to end the relationship - but the other person is still obsessively in love and won't let them go? What if that person stalks the client for the rest of his life?

* What if the client regrets his action, and wants to undo the love spell - and it can't be reversed?

* What if a paedophile uses love potions to seduce minors? What if a serial killer applies magic to lure victims to their doom?

* What if a fortune hunter tries to trick an heiress into drinking the love potion? What if she's been alerted to his intentions, and has to be constantly vigilant to thwart him?

* What if the family hires a bodyguard or detective to protect their heiress daughter from love spell assaults?

* What if the victim's family find out that the girl has been the victim of a love spell, and try to save her? What if they make great sacrifices to enable the spell to be undone - but she doesn't want to be saved?

* What if the heroine discovers that her best friend's intended is a ruthless man who forced her feelings with a love potion - and the friend refuses to believe it? What if the victim of the love spell is a man whom the heroine has secretly loved all her life, and now another woman has ensnared him with magic?

FURTHER READING

Love Magic by Laurie Cabot
Magical Love Spells by Lady Gianne

FOOD FOR THOUGHT

Have you ever been desperately in love, and the object of your affection did not want you? Recall how it felt. In this state of mind, would you have considered magical help? Would have listened to reason if a magician told you that it was unethical or unwise?

ASSIGNMENT

1. Test how well you know your magician character. If a client requests a love potion to win the heart of the girl he lusts after, what does she do? If she has scruples, what would make her set them aside and take the job? Would she use magic if her own passionate love is unrequited?

2. If your novel contains a love spell, or if you're thinking of adding one to the plot, tell us about it: Who is the client? Does it pose an ethical dilemma? What ingredients does she use?

3. Write a few paragraphs showing either the interaction between the magician and the client, or revealing the magician's ethical dilemma.

CHAPTER 10: SEX MAGIC

In real life, few magicians practice sex magic. In fiction, however, it offers exciting plot possibilities, especially if you write erotic novels with a paranormal edge, or paranormal novels with erotic spice.

If you find sex in fiction distasteful, simply skip this chapter.

POWER RAISING

Before casting a spell, a magician needs to create an intense flow of energy to fuel the magic. As discussed in Chapter 4, most do this with chanting, drumming or dancing. The magician in your story may do it with sex.

The power raised through sexual arousal can be phenomenal and serve to super-charge a spell. If your protagonist is a magician, you can use this for a plot-relevant erotic scene.

STRUCTURE OF THE RITUAL

1. The magician decides the desired outcome. Examples: make the crops grow, stop the flood, protect the traveller on a dangerous journey.

2. He plans and prepares the ritual. Examples: composing the words for the spell, assembling the ingredients, casting a circle around the area where the ritual will take place.

3. He gets into a state of sexual arousal - in any way which suits your story's plot.

4. Since the power is strongest immediately before orgasm, the magician tries to stretch out that phase for as long as possible.

5. In this state of intense arousal, he casts the spell. Example: he chants the words of the spell repeatedly. He concludes the spell with an assertion that this is his will. Example: a Wiccan witch may say 'So mote it be.'

6. Once the spell is cast, the ritual is over. To ground himself in reality again, he climaxes. For further grounding, he may eat or drink something.

7. He sleeps, exhausted by the combination of mental and physical exertion.

VARIATIONS

In some rituals, it's not the state of arousal, but the orgasm which fuels the magic.

Many rituals require a female/male pairing, others can be practised by same-gender couples as well. There are also rituals for groups.

Certain rituals require the exchange of body fluids (which means unprotected sex!) or simultaneous orgasms. These are typically practised by established couples, e.g. husband and wife teams.

PLOT POSSIBILITIES

Sex magic has drawbacks, complications and conflicts, which can make the story even more exciting.

Magic works through the mind and requires enormous concentration, which is difficult to achieve in a state of high arousal.

When two magicians join for sex magic, they can raise an enormous amount of power, but this requires them to synchronise their levels of arousal as well as their thoughts. This is unlikely to work for a couple who are not already established lovers.

However, you can use this near-impossibility to create tension: Perhaps the only way to save the world is through the kind of magic which requires intense power, and the only way to achieve so much power is for two magicians to work sex magic together. Will the heroine set aside her dislike of the hero and join him in the act? Unfamiliar with each other's bodies, can they coordinate their levels of arousal? The fictional possibilities are delicious.

Of course, solo sex magic with masturbation would be more practical, but it has less plot potential.

If you're writing erotic fiction, you could also use this for a BDSM scenario: a submissive person serves the dominant magician by arousing him to the desired level without causing distraction.

In a ménage scene, perhaps two magicians are an established team who have worked sex magic together on many occasions. A desperate situation requires additional energy, so they include a third person in their ritual. Will the new partner be able to synchronise his level of arousal with theirs? Excited by the presence of the new person, will the team be able to concentrate on the task?

In a state of arousal, judgement is impaired. A responsible magician never works magic on the spur of the moment while aroused, because he might be tempted to do something which is morally reprehensible or against his ethics.

For example, a male magician may fancy a woman like crazy, and the sight of her arouses him. In this state, he wants the woman - and he uses his arousal to cast a spell which will make her desire him with equal passion. By the time he comes to his senses, it's too late, and he may not be able to undo the spell. Maybe the woman divorces her loyal husband because she can no longer love him, or maybe the obsessed woman stalks the magician for the rest of his life.

Of course, in fiction it is interesting if a character makes a bad choice and has to deal with the consequences.

Sex magic leaves the magician tired, drained, and helpless. An enemy may use this vulnerable phase to attack the magician.

FURTHER READING

Celtic Sex Magic: For Couples, Groups, and Solitary Practitioners by Jon G. Hughes

Modern Sex Magick: Secrets of Erotic Spirituality by Donald Michael Kraig

ASSIGNMENT

1. What is your magician's stance on sex magic? Is it something he does as a matter of routine, something he would do if it made sense in a particular situation, something he would only consider in a dire emergency, or something so morally wrong that nothing could make him do it?

2. If sex magic suits your genre and plot, write a draft for a few paragraphs. Focus on the magician's need to raise power through arousal.

CHAPTER 11: MAGICAL WEAPONS AND WARFARE

When writing paranormal and fantasy fiction, we writers can invent fantastic weapons. However, these weapons need to be interesting so they enrich the story, and believable so the readers can suspend their disbelief.

A weapon which can kill anyone, any time, is implausible and boring.

Here are some ideas on how to create a magic weapon, inspired by real magic traditions from different cultures. Your weapon probably includes some, but not all, of these ideas. Have fun!

MATERIAL, SIZE AND SHAPE

* The weapon is made from a solid, natural material: stone, wood, or bone. The bone could be from a ritually sacrificed animal, from a human ancestor, from a hero or saint, or from a slain enemy.

* It may contain a crystal, or a precious or semi-precious stone, because these are good at storing and intensifying magical energy.

* It has an elongated shape, like a wand or a staff. Indeed, it may be disguised as an everyday elongated object, such as a pen or a walking stick. The magician points it at the target, similar to aiming a gun.

* The weapon can be of any size, from a tiny jewellery pendant to a tree trunk. Small items have the advantage that the magicians can carry them on their body or hide them in their garments. Large items may be stationary, and everyone knows of their existence and location.

* There is probably a religious connection. For example, the weapon may be sacred to a goddess, blessed in a temple, manufactured by monks, invented by a god, given to the hero by a goddess.

* It is probably old, perhaps inherited through generations.

* It can only be given - for example, in gratitude by the craftsman who made it, or granted by a priestess on her deathbed. It can't be bought with money.

* The manufacture of the weapon involved a ritual and a sacrifice. This may have been a human sacrifice. The weapon may have been dipped into the sacrificial victim's blood.

HOW IT WORKS

* Most magic works through the user's mind. To activate the weapon, the magician needs to concentrate, perhaps think a certain sequence of thoughts. The use of a magical weapon is never purely physical (such as pulling the trigger on a gun). It's the mental effort that counts. This can create interesting situations when the magician needs to concentrate to use the weapon, but can't concentrate in the heat of the battle.

* The damage inflicted by a magical weapon may be invisible. It may kill without leaving visible wounds, baffling the healers or coroners.

* Magical weapons may act slowly. A person may get hit by a magical weapon and not realise it until hours or days later, by which time it's too late to seek help.

* The weapon may affect the target's mind rather than the body. For example, it may rob that person of the will to live, or of the courage to fight.

* Many magical weapons work on one of the elements (earth, air, fire, water). For example, the weapon may kill by shaking the earth on which the target stands, or by heating the air the target breathes.

* The weapon can hit hidden targets. Its energy can move through or around obstacles.

* The user needs training to wield the weapon. This probably involves training in magic (power raising, mental focus, directing energy), as well as training in the use of the specific weapon. In the hands of an untrained person, the weapon may be ineffective, or may kill the user.

CHARGING AND CLEANSING

* Before use, the weapon needs to be magically fuelled (the usual term for this is 'charged'). This may be done in a certain place (at a spring, in a temple, at a crossroads) or by a certain person (a senior magician, a crone, a priestess). The charge involves a ritual, which may be simple or complex, and is often religious in nature. Sometimes, a weapon can be charged by leaving it lying in running water, or exposed to bright sunlight or to the light of the full moon. If the weapon contains a crystal, it's the crystal that gets charged.

* After use, the weapon needs to be ritually cleansed. This may be a simple act such as rinsing in running water, or it may need a prayer, or a complex ritual at the temple. The cleansing and the re-charging are often done in the same ritual.

PLOT POSSIBILITIES

Here are some ideas for spicing up your story with complications and conflicts:

* To be interesting, the weapon needs to have at least one weakness which causes difficulties for its user.

* After being ritually charged, the weapon works only for a specific period - perhaps for seven hours, or until the next new moon. After that period has passed, it may become inaccurate or less powerful, or stop working altogether.

* The weapon may only work in the hands of certain people: initiates of the order, male virgins, or post-menopausal crones. This can create interesting situations; for example, if it works only in the hands of a male virgin, the enemy may send a seductress.

* The weapon depends on the user's attitudes and beliefs. What if the weapon works only for a user whose religious faith is unshaken? (This would be especially appropriate for Religious Magic.) Or what if it only works for someone who is free from fear?

* In many magic traditions, the knowledge of names plays an important role. Perhaps the weapon works only if the user knows the target's true name.

* In some magic traditions, especially modern ones, visualisation is important. Perhaps the weapon works only if the user can visualise the target's face.

* The weapon may work only if the user is in a state of altered consciousness (i.e. in a trance); this can be tricky in a battle.

* Magic spells often take time. The user needs time to raise magical energy and to direct her will at the desired outcome. In an urgent fight situation, time may be short.

* Magic requires intense concentration. Perhaps this weapon needs several seconds of undistracted concentration before every shot.

* The weapon may work only in the presence of a certain element (earth, air, fire, water). For example, the user must stand near an open fire, or the target must be close to running water, otherwise it won't work.

HOW TO DEFEAT A MAGICIAN

Magic is mental work, and the magician's main weapon is his mind. If your PoV is a magician who fights with magic, he may struggle to concentrate while fighting.

If your PoV fights against a magician, she needs to ruin his concentration by creating distractions: talking, setting the curtains on fire, attacking him so fast he does not have time to think.

The best time to defeat a powerful magician is immediately after he has worked magic. Magic is mentally exhausting. It leaves the magician weak, tired and vulnerable. In this situation, your heroine can defeat the evil sorcerer.

The post-magic exhaustion can also create interesting plot situations if your magician hero has exhausted himself protecting others with his magic, and left himself open to attack.

MAGIC IN WARFARE

The magicians who work in the field of warfare are specialists. They are not the same magicians who brew love potions and vanquish warts.

There may be one single magician who acts as consultant to the commander-in-chief of the country's armed forces, or each legion may have its own magician. There may also be specialist magician units, as there are medical and engineering units. Normally, these magicians are involved in the battle preparations rather than in the actual fighting. However, units of magician-soldiers (trained in magic as well as in fighting) are plausible. These are likely to be either elite troops or auxiliaries.

In real societies where magic is practised, the magic plays an important role in the run-up to the battle. Magicians fulfil the roles of consultants, astrologers, prophets, psychologists and priests. They determine an auspicious date for the battle, assure the soldiers that fortune is on their side, bless the banners, call the favour of the gods on the weapons, lead prayers and read animal entrails for omens.

Magicians cannot bestow invincibility. However, they can create protective spells which deflect bullets, arrows and sword blows. These do not offer perfect protection and are no substitute for a Kevlar vest. They merely reduce the number and severity of hits, so the protected warrior still needs to carry a shield and duck fast.

The protection ritual takes time and energy to carry out. Shielding every soldier in an army of ten thousand with a protective spell is impractical. Perhaps only elite troops or only the officers are granted the treatment. This can lead to resentment among the grunt soldiers and create interesting sub-plots.

Protection spells take time; in a sudden ambush, the magician does not have time to create the protection for the soldier who had counted on it. They also wear off fast, which allows you to build tension if the battle lasts longer than the fighters expected, or if one fight follows another.

ASSIGNMENT

1. Invent a magical weapon, either for use in your story, or just for fun.

2. If your novel includes a scene in which a magician fights, write a paragraph for that fight scene. Show how the magician struggles to maintain his concentration.

CHAPTER 12: HEALING AND PROTECTION

Magicians with strict ethics often work in the fields of protection and healing.

HEALING

Healing magic is considered ethical even by the strictest standards. It's much practised in the contexts of Wiccan Witchcraft and Religious Magic.

Most religions have a form of healing magic - although they may not call it magic. Rather, they may use 'faith healing' and 'miracle'. Successful healing miracles can convince people of the validity of the religion, and encourage them to convert.

Shamanism involves a lot of healing magic, and it uses a holistic approach. Shamans believe that physical illness may have mental or spiritual causes, and they seek information and help from the spirit world.

The typical clients are sick people who suffer from painful chronic diseases. They have already tried conventional medicine, as well as complementary and alternative medicine, to no avail. Clients with terminal illnesses, such as advanced cancer, may do anything to prolong their lives.

The client could also be a friend or relative of the sick person, perhaps a mother desperate to save her newborn, or a husband whose wife is in permanent coma.

Although the magician should seek the patient's permission, this is not always possible. If the patient is unconscious, comatose or delirious, it's considered ethical to help them anyway.

Ethical dilemmas may arise, however, when a client seeks magical help for a sick person who doesn't want it. What if a mother would rather die and leave her young children orphaned, than accept help from a magician?

Most healing magic is subtle, strengthening the body's own immune defences so it can fight off infections, cancer cells and hormonal imbalances. Such subtle magic is often not recognised as magic, and the healing is attributed to other circumstances. This suits the patient and the magician well, because they don't wish to draw attention to the use of magic.

Dramatic, sudden healings - making a blind man see, enabling a paraplegic woman to leave her wheelchair and walk - attract a lot of attention. Some magicians welcome this publicity, especially faith healers seeking converts for their religion. Others shun it, because they'll inevitably get accused of being charlatans, and the patients will be derided as accomplices in the fraud.

Faith helps. The magic takes hold better if the patient believes in it, especially in Religious Magic (faith healing, miracles).

There may be psychological reasons for this (related to the placebo effect), it may be because the gods are more willing to help those who worship them, or it may be because faith makes the body more receptive to the magic.

In this context, you may consider the Bible story about Jesus healing the blind Bartimaeus as a form of Religious Magic. Note that Jesus says to the formerly blind man, "Go, your faith has helped you," making it clear that belief was an essential part of what happened.

In modern western society, medicine and magic are kept separate, and most medical professionals would be aghast at the thought of using magic to heal their patients.

This was not always so. In ancient Egypt, magicians appear to have practised medicine, and doctors to have practised magic. In other periods, the two fields also overlapped.

It's possible that in the future, magic and medicine will again join forces, and as a writer, you can create a world where this happens. For example, if you write science fiction, you can depict hospitals of the future which employ magicians among other medical specialists.

PROTECTION

Many people seek magical protection, and pay a magician to provide it.

For example, a farmer seeks to protect his crops against pests, a mother to protect her children against evil spirits, a courtesan to protect herself against curses from her lovers' wives, an adventurer to protect himself on a dangerous journey, a driver to protect his car against accidents, a home-owner to protect her house against lightning, a housewife to protect her larder against mice.

Ancient Egyptian Magic and Religious Magic especially provide people with magical protection.

When working protective magic, the magician usually casts a circle or oval around that person, sometimes physically (e.g. by sprinkling water, or by drawing a line in the sand), sometimes mentally (e.g. by visualising a circle of blue light).

The visualisation may also be a protective dome of light over the person. The magician may also give the client a protective amulet to wear.

GUARDING AGAINST HARMFUL MAGIC

Many modern magicians consider it an abomination to use magic to harm someone.

However, magicians of other cultures, periods and mindsets may not have the same qualms.

In a historical novel, it's quite possible that a magician accepts the job of hexing or cursing someone, as long as the client pays well.

Hexes and curses

A harmful spell is called a 'hex' or a 'curse'. The definitions of the two overlap, but here are the approximate explanations:

* A hex is worked in cold blood, unemotionally, while a curse involves intense emotions such as righteous fury.

* A hex lasts a few hours, days or weeks, and then wears off, while a curse lasts a lifetime and sometimes generations.

* A hex is usually Low Magic, while a curse may be High Magic.

* A hex is always worked by a magician, while a curse can sometimes be worked by a non-magician.

* A hex is usually secular, while a curse often has a religious element (e.g. the spell caster curses in the name of a deity).

* A hex can affect an object or a person, while a curse always affects a person, or a group of people.

* Hexes tend to cause great nuisance, but not long-term harm, while curses bring long-term devastating harm.

Protection against magical attacks

Many people who believe they've been cursed or hexed are merely suffering a stroke of bad luck, or have a bout of karma catching up with them, or may even be simply paranoid. A psychic may be best equipped to give a proper diagnosis, disputing or confirming the existence of a magical attack, and possibly pinpointing its source.

The afflicted person may then seek the help of a magician to stop the attack.

A magician cannot normally undo another magician's spell. However, she can deflect its power, and she can make the victim less vulnerable.

The ritual seeks to deflect the harm. It often involves creating a circle of mirrors around the victim. The mirrors reflect the hex or curse, and send it back to the sender.

Wiccan witches believe that any harm gets returned to the sender anyway: a magician who works curses or hexes will suffer exactly the same fate she wished on the victim, or the same fate threefold or ninefold or a hundredfold, depending on which branch of Wicca the believer belongs to. Other modern magicians don't quite believe this, but consider it possible, and this fear is enough to keep them from causing harm.

In the case of a curse, the magician will ask the victim to do a favour or give a gift to the person who cursed them. The victim may balk at this request, but it really lessens the power of the curse.

To reduce the harm from the curse or hex, and to protect the victim from further attacks, the magician will probably provide an amulet.

TALISMANS AND AMULETS

Talisman and amulets give magical energy to the people who wear them, including people who are not magicians. They are two different magical objects, and it's best not to confuse them, although the definitions overlap sometimes.

To decide whether the magical item is a talisman or an amulet, consider the following:

* An amulet gives general help, while a talisman serves one specific purpose.

* An amulet keeps harm away, while a talisman empowers the wearer.

* An amulet is mostly secular in nature, while a talisman typically contains divine, angelic or spirit energy.

* An amulet deflects negative energies, while a talisman attracts positive ones.

* An amulet usually works for whoever wears it, while a talisman is often custom-made for one particular person.

However, these definitions are fluid. Choose the one which suits your magical artefact best, and stick with it.

Amulets and talismans need to be close to the person they empower or protect. Usually, they are worn as pendants on the chest. However, they could also be carried in the hand or in the pocket, hung from a car's rear-view mirror or placed under a sleeper's pillow.

Although they can be of any shape, they are often round. Pendants are typically metal disks, set with a gemstone and engraved with mystic symbols. They may also take the shape of a small pouch, filled with symbolic ingredients such as herbs, coins, crystals, bones, relics, pieces of pages from the religion's holy book, or miniature statues of the protective deity.

In some cultures, amulets and talismans were worn as finger rings.

The maker is always a magician of sorts. She either makes it herself, for example, by filling the small pouch with herbs and symbolic items), or commissions an artisan (for example, a silversmith to create a disk-shaped pendant) which she then charges magically.

The best time to charge an amulet is during the waning moon, while for talismans the waxing moon is best.

Most amulets work automatically all the time. Some talismans, however, need activating. When the need arises, the wearer must do something to release its power. For example, she must say certain words, turn her finger ring, or rub the disk.

In ancient Egypt, amulets were big business. The average person in the street would wear several amulets for protection against all sorts of dangers. Archaeologists have found amulets which appear to have been mass-produced in factories, and it seems likely that many magicians earned their bread and butter by charging amulets. Wealthy people preferred custom-made amulets over mass-manufactured ones.

FURTHER READING

Amulets & Talismans for Beginners: How to Choose, Make & Use Magical Objects by Richard Webster

Magic's in the Bag: Creating Spellbinding Gris Gris Bags & Sachets by Jude Bradley and Cheré Dastugue Coen

Death and Destruction: How to Cast Magic Spells for Vengeance, Harm, &c. by Talia Felix

Protection and Reversal Magick by Jason Miller

Body Guards: Protective Amulets & Charms by Desmond Morris

Practical Protection Magick: Guarding & Reclaiming Your Power by Ellen Dugan

FOOD FOR THOUGHT

1. Do you, or does someone you know, wear or carry a charm, amulet, talisman, religious medal or similar object? Where does it come from, who made it, what does it protect from or guard against?

2. Have you read a work of fiction involving an amulet, a talisman, a curse or a hex? Tell us about it.

ASSIGNMENT

1. What is your magician character's stance on curses and hexes? Under which circumstances would she use magic to harm someone?

2. If your story has an amulet or a talisman, describe it to us: What is it made of, what does it look like, who made it, what are its powers?

CHAPTER 13: ETHICS, CONFLICTS, SECRECY

In this chapter, you'll gain some ideas on how to add depth and tension to your story.

ETHICS

Magicians of all systems, cultures and periods have strong views of what's right and what's wrong. However, these principles vary.

21st century western magicians consider it highly unethical to use magic to harm someone. But in most periods of history, harmful spells (curses and hexes) were big business, often the magician's main source of income. Clients paid good money to have their enemies and rivals hexed.

Wiccan witches consider it unethical to interfere with a person's free will, so love spells for making someone fall in love without their consent are forbidden. But in historical periods, many Traditional witches earned their main income brewing love potions, and saw nothing wrong with it.

Most High magicians would never work magic under the influence of alcohol or mind-altering drugs. But many shamans only ever work magic under the influence.

Since ethical rules vary so greatly, you can be creative and invent some for your novel. Just give your magician some strong ethical principles.

These principles may be prescribed by the professional association the magician belongs to, or by the branch of magic, or by the period, or they may be individual choices. They may be quietly held beliefs, or they may be codes which the initiate has to swear by before he is accepted into the guild. It may be a single rule, or a set of three or seven or twelve, or it can be a catalogue of five hundred which the apprentice has to learn by heart.

For fiction, a magician's ethics are wonderful plot fodder. Early in the novel, establish that there's something your magician hero would never do. In the middle of the novel, tempt him to do it, but allow him to stay firm. At the novel's climax, he has to decide between this principle and another, equally important one. This will have the reader on the edge of his seat, wondering what the magician will do.

Villainous Ethics

You can have real fun with your villain's ethics. His principles are just as strong as the hero's, they're just ... different.

Here are some ideas:

* "Never torture someone on a Sunday."
* "Perform harmful spells only when the moon is full."
* "Don't interfere with someone's free will unless the client pays in gold."

Or maybe he has his own way of interpreting the principles.

* "Never hurt an animal." (= Hurting a human is OK)

* "Never hurt someone over the age of seventy" (= Get your hands on that crone before she reaches that birthday)

* "Never harm a child under twelve" (= Snatch that eleven-year-old and keep him prisoner until his birthday)

* "Never attack another magician" (= Attack his helpless wife instead)

* "Never harm a virgin" (= ensure she's no longer a virgin)

* "Don't kill" (= get your minions to do the killing for you)

The Wiccan Rede

Among modern magicians, the most widely followed ethic principle is, "Do what you want, as long as it harms none." This is written in different ways, for example "An it harm none, do what ye will." (The Wiccan Rede).

As well as Wiccans, most New Age magicians adhere to a variation of it, and they may defend it passionately.

However, there is a lot of disagreement over what it means. The word 'an' (sometimes rendered 'er') in particular causes puzzlement. There has been much learned discourse, even more unlearned speculation, and great heat under cauldrons.

Allegedly, the principle is an old one, going back to pre-Christian Celtic traditions. This may or may not be true. The Celtic witches didn't write things down, and the oral history is more than doubtful, especially since New Age leaders are very good at inventing ancient traditions. Accordingly, scholars have turned to Celtic and Anglo Saxon languages to define what 'an' or 'er' means, and they don't agree whether it means 'if' or 'because', or something else. Some say that 'an' and 'er' are simply gibberish.

If 'an' means 'because' or 'since', the principle seems to assure the practitioner that whatever they do, it won't harm anyone. Therefore, they can do what they like, without harmful side effects.

If, on the other hand, 'an' means 'if', the meaning is very different: "As long as it doesn't harm anyone, you may proceed."

Therefore: "You may proceed only if you're absolutely sure that this is not going to harm anyone in any way."

This limits a magician's scope. It stops the magician from working curses and hexes.

If a magician really thinks this through, it may stop him from working any magic at all. Even apparently benevolent magic causes harm to someone. Anything benefiting one person is likely to be to the detriment of another.

For example, a magician heals a fatally ill woman. When she is well and returns to work, a desperate unemployed person is deprived of a job opportunity.

Or perhaps the magician helps a barren woman conceive. But that child grows up to be Adolf Hitler.

Whatever magic a magician works, it will have direct and indirect consequences, many of them bad.

Perhaps this is the purpose of the Wiccan Rede: not to dictate what the magicians may do, but to make them consider the effects their actions may have on others.

Wannabe magicians often focus on 'do what you will' and ignore the clause 'as long as it harms none'. It's a licence to bypass restrictions, and just have fun unhampered by morals.

SECRECY

Many magicians keep quiet about their trade, because they fear the disapproval, distrust and hostility of other people.

In some periods, magic was outlawed, and the penalties for practising magic were severe. In the Middle Ages, being convicted (or even just suspected) of being a witch meant torture and execution. The execution method varied - in some countries, witches were hanged, in others burned at the stake. If writing medieval historical fiction, make sure you get this right.

Religious Magic is especially problematic if the magician's faith isn't the dominant, government-sanctioned belief. Religious leaders and their followers are quick to denounce other religions' magicians as evil sorcerers who worship the devil, and often get them arrested, tortured and executed.

Even in societies where magic is permitted and respectable, there remains a lingering worry about the magician's mysterious powers. Neighbours may avoid close contact, parents may not permit their kids sleepovers in the magician's house.

Rumours spread, often based on people's worst fears: The couple who live in the house opposite are Wiccan witches. Does this mean they worship the devil? Do they sacrifice children? There's loud music coming from that house, surely this means there's a satanic orgy going on. And the candles burning in their living room are sure proof of a black mass!

Overall, most magicians find it safer and pleasanter simply not to reveal what they do. Only a small circle of friends, and other magicians of the same system, are aware.

In societies where magic is forbidden and punished, every magician is constantly worried about whom he may trust. One single error in judgement can cost his life, and that of his friends. This may force magicians to be secretive and can make them feel lonely.

If your magician characters meet in secret, they probably wear everyday clothes, so they don't stand out. Alternatively, they may wear cloaks to hide their faces, preferably in dark grey or black which make the wearer almost invisible in a crowd.

In the western world, Wiccan witches are the most open about what they do. They have websites, they wear pentagram pendants, they campaign for religious freedom, and spread information. They have done a lot of good work in dismantling public prejudice and fear, and Wiccan Witchcraft has become almost mainstream. However, many people still view Wiccan witches with deep distrust.

WHEN MAGES MAKE MISTAKES - PLOT POSSIBILITIES

Magicians are fallible like other humans.

You can create exciting plot complications if the magician who casts a spell gets it wrong.

Other books on magic teach you how to get magic right - but for a writer, magic going wrong is far more useful.

Here are some ideas you can use in your fiction.

* The magician summons a spirit (e.g. a demon) to do his bidding - but that spirit is malevolent and more powerful than he expected, and he is unable to keep it under control.

* The magician creates a protective circle around himself which shields him from the summoned spirits and from evil - but then he accidentally steps out of the circle.

* The magician recites a complicated spell ... but he misremembers a word or mispronounces a syllable, and the outcome is not what he intended. (This happens only with forms of magic which rely on the precise wording, for example, Ancient Egyptian magic. It doesn't happen with forms of magic where the intent is more important than the word, such as Wiccan Witchcraft.)

* The magician wants something intensely, and doesn't mean to cast a spell ... but he has unwittingly raised magical energy by dancing or drumming, and his intense desire turns into a spell... one which he comes to regret bitterly.

* The magician, roused to righteous anger, casts a harmful spell (a hex or a curse) on someone... but the harm returns to him, and he suffers the same fate. (In some forms of magic, it is said that the harm returns threefold, ninefold, or a hundredfold.)

* The magician casts a benevolent spell to help someone... but by helping one person, he is harming another (e.g. by helping a friend succeed at a job interview, he robs someone else of the chance), and the harm returns to him.

* The magician casts a spell on the spur of the moment, which at the time seems the right thing to do... but afterwards, he realises that what he has done is unethical, or has unwanted consequences.

* The magician summons a god into the circle ...., but gods don't take kindly to humans who boss them about. Although they may lend a helping hand to the magician who invites them, they may punish the presumptuous ones.

* The magician raises magical energy to fuel a spell (for example, by dancing, drumming or chanting)... but he raises more than he intended, and the spell magnifies out of proportion. He may intend to light a candle, and instead he sets the house on fire. He may intend to bring an afternoon's sunshine, and instead he brings ten years of desperate drought.

* The magician may desperately try to concentrate on the spell, because magic works through the mind... but in a situation of acute danger, he can't concentrate.

The more urgently he needs to concentrate, the less he is able to. Perhaps the gun-armed killers are already breaking down the door, or the sadistic villain is torturing his lover in the same room, and the distraction means he can't summon the concentration he needs to work magic.

* The magician casts a spell for what he wants to happen... but he forgets to specify how. For example, if he's desperate for cash, he may cast a spell for a hundred thousand dollars, and a week later he learns that his beloved sister has died and left him that amount in her will.

* The magician casts a spell for what he wants to happen... but he forgets to specify when. The results come years later, when he has long forgotten about the spell, and when the results are no longer desirable.

Magical mistakes can seldom be undone. Trying to undo a spell may even mess things up further.

A sensible, experienced magician will always think carefully before she works magic, considering the necessary preparations, the ethical implications and the possible consequences - but the magician in your novel may not always be careful and sensible.

OUTER CONFLICT - PLOT POSSIBILITIES

Ethics, secrecy and errors create conflict which can add tension to your story. Here are some ideas.

Outer conflict

* The government or the dominant religion persecutes magicians (e.g. witch-hunts), so if he is discovered, he may be tortured or killed. Therefore, he must practice his craft in secret.

* Magic is illegal, so by practising magic, the magician commits a crime and is at conflict with the law.

* Society believes that all magicians are evil, or devil worshippers, or sacrificing children in their rituals, so people shun the magician.

* Many people are frightened of the magician's abilities and don't trust him; this makes it difficult to make true friends. Perhaps he likes someone, or even falls in love, but either he or that person doesn't dare to trust.

* Some may seek to ingratiate themselves with the magician in the hope of gaining benefits; the magician may realise that the person he thought was a friend was just taking advantage.

* Friends expect the magician to solve their problems magically. They may not accept that the magician is unable to, or that ethical considerations prevent him.

* Whenever something bad happens in the neighbourhood, the magician gets the blame ("He put the curse on my cow!" "He gave my daughter the measles by looking at her")

* Family, friends, a spouse or a lover exerts pressure on the magician to switch to a different form of magic (from secular to religious magic, or from an exotic form to mainstream, or from a minority religion to the dominant religion).

* Family, friends, a spouse or a lover exert pressure to give up magic altogether.

* The professional organisation to which the magician belongs uses magic in ways the magician considers unethical (e.g. production of magical weapons of mass destruction), and exerts pressure on the magician to get involved.

* The professional organisation disapproves of the magician's work and threatens to expel him, to withdraw his licence, or to punish him.

* Two magicians are in competition: perhaps there's only enough business for one witch in the village, or only one can get and keep the job of magical advisor to the king.

-* A rival magician spreads rumours and lies about him in order to undermine his position.

* He gets accused of being a charlatan or a fake.

* In order to move up in the hierarchy of magicians and attain a prestigious post, he must learn new skills and pass challenges which are beyond his current abilities.

* The ruler of the land is a magician and has to use magic to defend the land.

* Unscrupulous people try force the magician to work evil magic on their behalf.

INNER CONFLICTS - PLOT POSSIBILITIES

* The magician may not want to be a magician because he considers it morally wrong, but he has natural ability which manifests itself.

* The magician lives in a magic-phobic society and wonders whether to come out of the closet.

* He feels a strong calling to be a magician, but he is devoutly religious, and his religion forbids magic.

* His needs could be fulfilled with magic, but they clash with his ethics (e.g. the woman he loves doesn't reciprocate his feelings. With a spell, he could make her love him. But interfering with another person's free will is unethical).

* He could alleviate another person's suffering with magic, but only if he breaks an oath and uses magic the way it's not meant to be used. (e.g. an unemployed person desperately needs a job, and would get one if the rival dropped out. The magician could make the rival sick on interview day, so the needy person gets the job. But causing harm to someone is against magical ethics.)

I recommend choosing at least one inner and one or two outer conflicts. These can be in addition to non-magical conflicts your story explores. Choose conflicts which suit your story, your genre, your period, and your character. If possible, select conflicts which illustrate or enhance your novel's theme.

FOOD FOR THOUGHT

1. Have you read a work of literature in which a magician's ethics play a role? Are these ethics prescribed by a magical organisation, or do they originate from the magician's individual values?

2. Do you have any fun ideas for a villainous sorcerer's ethics?

ASSIGNMENT

1. What are your magician character's ethical principles? In what way do they create a dilemma for him?

2. In your fiction, what is society's attitude towards magicians?

3. Give the magician in your story an ethical dilemma.

CHAPTER 14: ILLUSIONISTS AND CHARLATANS

A 'magician' who doesn't work real magic but entertains the audience with baffling tricks is called an 'illusionist', while a faker who claims to work real magic but doesn't is a 'charlatan'.

Sometimes, the lines between magicians, illusionists and charlatans are blurred, and this can make great material for fiction.

ILLUSIONISTS

What They Do

Illusionists perform 'magic' tricks to amaze onlookers, either for fun or for money. Many hire themselves out as entertainers for children's parties, village fêtes, cabarets, variety shows and other events.

Broadly speaking, there are two types of modern illusionism: stage magic and close-up magic.

In stage magic, the entertainer performs acts which can be witnessed by a large audience from a distance, such as levitating a person, or sawing a lady in in half. Often, these involve mechanical apparatus.

In close-up magic, she entertains a smaller group with card tricks or by pulling coins from someone's nose. These are mostly sleight-of-hand.

How It's Done

Here are some techniques illusionists use often:

* Sleight of hand. These are skilled deceptions achieved by manual dexterity and speed, used especially for card tricks.

*Misdirection. A showy action draws the spectators' eyes, so they don't notice what else is going on. While the spectators watch one hand, the other hand acts swiftly and unseen. The magician's glamorous assistant often draws attention to herself.

* Thumb-tips. A flesh-coloured cap fits over the thumb. Inside it, small objects can be hidden. This method works especially well for producing and vanishing handkerchiefs (called 'silks') which are so thin that, when crumpled, they fit into the smallest space.

* Mirrors. A mirror acts as an invisible dividing wall behind which something can be hidden. For example, the illusionist pours a liquid into a glass beaker divided by a mirror, so the front half is full and the back half is empty.

* The colour black. A black object is invisible if it moves in front of a black background. The back of the stage is often black, so the audience doesn't see the black apparatus move. Illusionists may also wear black suits, and use boxes and bags with black insides.

* Double bottoms, double layers and double doors. Most of the equipment the illusionist uses has double walls, usually painted black. When she opens a door or shows the inside of something, there's usually another door or bottom in front of or behind it.

Some professional organisations make their members swear not to reveal to non-members how something is done. However, these oaths have become largely obsolete, because instruction books and DVDs are widely available, YouTube videos reveal the techniques, and websites show how to work tricks step-by step.

It matters little, because knowledge doesn't equal skill. Knowing that a handkerchief can fit into a thumb-tip isn't enough to perform the illusion. Only many hours of diligent practice allow the illusionist to pull it off. Sometimes, knowing how it's done actually increases the spectator's respect for the illusionist's skill.

Psychological Profile of an Illusionist

When creating an illusionist character, you may want to use some or all of these features: psychologically astute, skilled with her fingers, experienced entertainer, good at lying (though not necessarily using this ability), curious, diligent, determined, patient, charismatic.

Modern illusionists may call themselves 'magicians', but they don't pretend that they work real magic. Instead, they impress audiences with ingenuity and skill.

In historical periods, however, they would often fool gullible spectators into believing that it was real magic, so as to earn more money. This would make them charlatans. They could earn more if naive spectators thought they were witnessing magic, so there may not have been a separation between illusionists and charlatans.

CHARLATANS

Some people pretend to work magic, although they can't. They do this to impress their peers, to scare their enemies, to pull chicks, to prop up their image, to make religious converts, or to earn money.

Real magician tend to ignore charlatans, but sometimes they get angry because charlatans give real magic a bad name.

<u>Psychological Profile of a Charlatan.</u>

These fakers often wear flashy clothes in black and purple, with lots of mystic symbols and big pendants.

They may boast a lot and mention their magical powers at every opportunity. A charlatan is probably a good liar, with low or flexible ethical standards, and she may have a cynical attitude or low self-worth. Some charlatans are greedy.

<u>Religious Charlatans</u>

Charlatans also operate in the field of Religious Magic, pretending to work miracles in order to attract followers, to frighten wrong-doers away from sin, or to prove that their god is real. A startling miracle can turn sinners into righteous people, and unbelievers into converts. When the deity doesn't deliver the desired miracle, the priests may resort to trickery.

In Alexandria in first century AD, society was religiously tolerant, and many faiths - Greek and Egyptian religion, Mithraism, Zoroastrianism, Judaism and more - co-existed peacefully. However, the temples were in fierce competition for worshippers, each aiming to outdo the others with miracles to wow potential converts. The more spectacular the show, the more people flocked to the temple.

Since the gods did not oblige with constant miracles, the priests commissioned inventors and engineers to build clever automatons. With the help of magnetism, hydraulics, steam and other technology, chariots were made to fly overhead, statues to pour wine, figures to swivel, dance and kiss. One of history's most famous inventors, Hero of Alexandria, made a career of supplying miracle automatons to temples.

Blurred Lines

Sometimes, the line between 'real magic' and 'fake magic' is a thin one, especially when a real magician supplements real magic with fakery.

Here are some fictional scenarios in which a real magician resorts to fakery:

1. Mightus the Great, King of Medievalia, invites all magicians in the land to audition for the post of Court Wizard. It's a prestigious job, superbly paid, and Magus Aspirus really wants it. Part of the audition involves levitating the emperor's goblet. Magus Apirus can do that in his sleep. But he wants to stand out from the crowd of applicants. So, when his turn comes, he uses sleight of hand and misdirection to set off fireworks, while his hidden accomplice creates smoke, smells and noises. Then he levitates the goblet. When Mightus the Great makes his choice, he remembers Magus Aspirus. Although Aspirus didn't lift the goblet very high, his act looked like real magic to Mightus. Aspirus gets the job.

2. A witch in 18th century London specialises in magic to keep husbands faithful. Her ready-made brew is potent but looks plain, and when she decants it, the clients doubt that it's real magic.

So the witch invites the client into a darkened room, chants ominously while she stirs her cauldron, adds drops which changes the purple brew's colour to green or red, and sprinkles a mysterious powder which makes the liquid foam and hiss. Now the witch decants the potion, and the client goes away happily impressed and confident of the magic's power. The potion is the same, merely dyed with red cabbage; the added ingredients are harmless natural substances such as lemon juice which caused a visible chemical reaction and have no magical effect whatsoever.

3. Miraculous healings at the site of the martyred St. Holya draw throngs of pilgrims.

The town's inns flourish, the monks in the monastery brew St. Holya wine and local sellers do a brisk trade in St. Holya statuettes and other souvenirs. Then the miracles cease. The local economy collapses as sick pilgrims seek salvation elsewhere. Intense prayers to St. Holya to please resume the miracles bring no result, so the monks take a drastic measure. They hire an able-bodied beggar to limp into the church on St. Holya's feast day, kiss the statue's feet, and throw away his crutches. Word spreads, and the pilgrimage business revives.

PLOT POSSIBILITIES

* What if an illusionist accidentally works real magic during a public performance?

* What if a greedy charlatan fools audiences into thinking him a real magician... and one day the deity or demon he invokes decides to teach him a lesson?

* What if an illusionist encourages audiences to believe that he is working real magic... and then religious fanaticism sweeps the land, the inquisition hunts, tortures and kills magicians, and nobody believes him when he says that he lied?

* What if a devout young priest discovers that the pilgrimage site stages fake miracles, and his superiors are in on the scam? What if speaking up would get him kicked out of the priesthood?

* The Bible tells of how the prophet Elijah challenged the priests of Baal: he and they would each build an altar and pray to their deity to set the altar on fire. Elijah's prayer was answered with fire from heaven, and the worshippers left Baal for Jehovah. What if another group of pagan priests demands a repetition of the experiment? What if they've learnt from experience that Baal won't help, so they prep the altar with naphta and limestone, which, when water is added, will burst into flame?

* What if an inventor in ancient Alexandria feels qualms of conscience about creating fake miracles?

* What if the competition between the temples turns nasty, and the priests try to expose a rival temple's miracles?

* What if a goddess gets angry at the charlatan priests who create fake miracles in her name?

* What if an actor who pretended to be a cured cripple blackmails the miracle preacher, threatening to expose the fake?

ASSIGNMENT

1. Does your magician ever use illusionism? Why and how?

2. Could your story involve a charlatan? What kind of magic might he pretend to do? How does the real magician react to this?

CHAPTER 15: MAGIC IN THE FUTURE

In the modern western word, most people don't believe that magic exists - but throughout history, humans have believed in and used magic. What if the current disbelief is a temporary phase, and in the future, magic becomes an established fact?

Most likely, magic will become a scientific discipline, studied, researched and used for commercial and military purposes.

You can have fun imagining a world where magic has become mainstream. This will work especially well for science fiction, urban fantasy and steampunk.

Here are some ideas to get your creative juices flowing. You're welcome to use any of them in your story, or you may treat them as inspiration to develop your own.

FUTURE MAGIC SCENARIOS

* Universities have departments of magic, offering degrees in subjects such as magical anthropology, magical energy studies, comparative magic and magical theology.

* Research magicians apply for grants from the government.

* Hospitals employ healing magicians the same way they employ surgeons and scrub nurses.

* People hire self-employed mages to fix their problems the way they hire plumbers and handymen.

* Celebrity magicians get interviewed on television talk shows.

* Teams of mages compete in televised contests.

* Nations have laws about proper and improper uses of magic. (Heavy penalties for using magic against royals, and for interfering with a minor's free will)

* Magic is used to power engines and telecommunication.

* MRI scans detect what results magic activity has on the brain.

* Some psychotherapists specialise in treating magic-traumatised victims.

* A large part of each nation's military budget goes towards magical weapons and defences.

* The army, navy and air force have magician units.

* Large-scale studies compare the effectiveness of different spells and different magic systems on different people, complete with control groups and placebos.

* Magicians seek publication in peer-reviewed journals.

* Environmentalists advocate the use of magic instead of fossil fuel.

* After decades of unrestricted magic use, humans become aware that magic has harmful effects on the environment. By that time, Earth suffers the consequences of heavy magic pollution.

* Unprotected exposure to large doses of magic is harmful. ('The patient's condition is critical after suffering third degree magic burns.')

* In some areas, use of magic is so frequent that the concentration of magical energies leads to problems: pets display disturbed behaviour, wildlife fail to reproduce, and homing pigeons lose their way.

* Some churches teach scientific methods of prayer to best harness the power of magic.

* There are units for measuring the intensity and speed of magic. ('The spell registered seven degrees on the Murray scale, with a speed of 220 Cunningham.')

* Instead of finding witchcraft cool, teenagers moan about having to study magic in school.

* Software and apps enable ordinary people to use magic on their computers.

* Some forms of magic interfere with Wifi and mobile phone signals (or whatever communication methods are used in the future).

* When people think about the 20th and 21st century, they shake their heads at the ignorance of a population that was ninety-nine percent magic-illiterate.

* In some countries, denying the existence of magic is a punishable offence.

* In totalitarian states, all magic is controlled by the government. Anyone found practising magic without permission gets imprisoned.

* Only holders of accredited qualifications may practice magic.

FOOD FOR THOUGHT

In a future world where magic has become mainstream, how would it affect your job, your leisure, your daily routines?

ASSIGNMENT

1. If your story is set in a future period, a secondary world or an alternate universe, identify the scenarios which may apply.

2. In what other ways might magic be 'normal' in your fiction world?

CHAPTER 16: FICTION SAMPLES

Here are two samples from my own writing, to show how I've used magic in my fiction. Perhaps you enjoy my writing style, perhaps you don't; either way, you may find it interesting to see how I've put the theory into writing practice.

SHORT STORY: BY YOUR OWN FREE WILL

by Rayne Hall

Ms Marian Meer, MBA, wondered how much the love potion would cost. Prices probably varied with the clients' need for the product, so she must act cool and not let the witch guess her despair.

Sharlene Ravenheart Shoenickle, read the small brass plate. *Consultations by appointment.* Marian pressed the bell, straightened her jacket cuffs and waited.

The door swished open, revealing a woman of around forty swathed in tie-dyed green, lilac and purple who beckoned her in with silver-ringed fingers. "Come, sit on the couch here. I've brewed us some nice chamomile tea."

The room smelled of beeswax and frankincense. Marian cast a quick glance around to assess the place.

Layered ethnic rugs on the floor, walls covered in posters of female deities, bunches of dried herbs hanging from the rafters: a New Ager.

Shelves crammed with books like *Wicca 333 - Advanced Topics in Wiccan Belief, Shamanism and Witchcraft - A Comprehensive Study* and *Magic - A Historical Perspective:* academic approach to her subject, educated at college level or above.

Two couches piled with cushions, a desk with a computer and filing cabinet: living room and workplace in one. Purple velvet curtains faded at the edges, chipped earthenware mugs, a desktop computer with the kind of boxy monitor common a decade ago: money was tight.

Ringbinders labelled with dates: in business for ten years or more. A playpen in the back of the room: a single mum working from home, where she could keep an eye on her offspring whenever she couldn't arrange childcare.

Having ascertained Ms Shoenickle's situation, Marian was ready for the negotiation. She cleared a pile of mismatched cushions to the side and lowered herself on the couch.

"Help yourself to sugar. It's fair-traded and unrefined," the witch chirped. "Is this the first time you've consulted a witch?"

"It is, but you can skip the preliminaries. I know what I want."

"Why don't you try my organic oats flapjack, dear? Or the wholemeal gingerbread?"

"Can we get to business, please? I have to be back in the office at one. I want a standard love potion to give to one specific man."

Ms Shoenickle clicked her tongue. "I don't deal in love potions. I'm a respectable witch."

Marian waved aside that price-inflating ploy. "Here's my card."

The business card said *Marian Meer, MBA, Senior Data Analyst, Groneagle & Co, Mensa Member.* The mention of Mensa always gained respect and cut through a lot of small talk. But the witch barely gave the card a glance.

"I've researched the topic," Marian said briskly. "I know that love potions have been witches' stock-in-trade throughout history. How much do you charge?"

The witch heaped brown sugar into her cup and stirred. "Interfering with someone's feelings and free will is unethical. Here's a better idea. I'll cast a general spell to invite love into your life. How about that, dear?"

"You don't understand." Marian plunked her cup down. "I don't want general love, I want Josh. No one else can make me complete."

"If he wants to be with you, he'll come to you. Nothing good comes from forcing love."

"Yes, yes, I'm sure you're right, for normal affairs. But this is different! This is real love, not a crush. We've been colleagues for years, he really likes me... just not in the right way. We're meant to be together. I know it! All I need is a potion to make him feel our love."

The witch made a clucking noise and shook her head. "Unwilling love doesn't make good relationships. It can lead to great pain."

"Once he loves me, he'll be happy."

Still the witch stirred her tea, with the spoon pinched between her forefinger and thumb, purple nails gleaming. "I can see that your feelings for him are strong."

"They are! He's my soulmate. We have so much in common- we both practice Hatha Yoga, we both eat lean meat, we both read Sartre. We're teetotallers and we don't touch nicotine or drugs. Our temperaments are perfect complements. He's gentle where I'm firm, diplomatic where I'm focused, earth where I'm water. It's clear we're meant for each other. You simply have to help me. I need this man!"

"Drink your tea, dear. It'll make you feel calmer."

Marian straightened. She hadn't meant to reveal her need. Displaying emotion was always a mistake - people thought you were weak.

The witch hadn't said that a love spell was impossible, only that she didn't want to do it. This meant she was open to negotiation.

A piercing wail came from the playpen.

"That's Daniel," the witch said. "Will you excuse me for a moment?" Before Marian could reply, the witch dashed to the pen, bent over the rail and cooed something at her baby.

Marian nodded to herself. She had had dealings with single mums before, including the type that worked from home. Neither sense nor scruples stopped them from getting what was best for the child.

Marian would achieve her goal after all. The child was the lever. At once, she rose and joined her hostess, adopting the sweet singsong voice she had heard women use around small ones. "How old is your Daniel?"

"Daniel is twelve."

"Twelve? But he's still in the -" The shocked words escaped from Marian's mouth before she could stop them.

The witch hoisted the child out of the playpen. A big body with sagging limbs, vacant eyes, saliva drooling. Disgust and pity mixed in Marian's chest.

Hastily, she tried to cover her mistake with an innocuous remark: "He...he's..b-big for his age." But that was an even more stupid thing to say. Embarrassment heated Marian's cheeks.

Better not say anything else and let Ms Shoenickle take the lead. The witch had been in this business for over a decade, and assuming she saw around twenty clients per week, she had to have experienced a good many insensitive remarks.

Marian averted her gaze so she needn't watch how the mother patted the child and muttered to him until the wailing ceased. Clearly, she loved him, and had chosen to raise him at home, presumably at great personal sacrifice. Most likely, the husband had deserted on the arrival of the idiot child. As a single mum working from home, she wouldn't be able to afford professional care.

Marian, on the other hand, had money. As a senior analyst with Groneagle & Co, she drew a substantial annual salary. She had a savings account, a flat in the City, and no dependants.

"Help me with my problem, and I'll pay enough to hire an attendant for Daniel, so he gets the professional care he deserves," she tempted. "Isn't this a win-win situation for all three of us?"

The witch lowered the child back into the playpen and returned to the couch. "Let's talk about it." She was speaking slowly, thoughtfully, stroking her chin. "You're sure you want this man? You would give what it takes to win his love?"

Marian sat and leant forward in a pose that encouraged negotiations, with her palms turned up and an assuring smile on her face. "I've thought it through. Now it's a matter how much money you need. How about one year's salary for a private nurse with the right qualifications?"

"Money can't buy what Daniel needs." Sharlene picked the business card from the table and twisted it between her fingers. "Mensa member. This means your IQ is 140?"

Marian smiled some more. "Mine is 163, actually, on the Stanford Binet scale."

"And the average human's is 100, right?"

"Depending on the scale used."

The witch's chest heaved, lifting the chunky pendant up and down. "Then what are you using the extra 63 for? Do you need them for your job? Do they make you happy?"

Marian indulged her curiosity. "My kind of job requires more than average intelligence," she explained, "although hardly 163. Most of my colleagues have 120, 130 maybe."

Except Josh. Josh was a Mensa member, too, and his mind was superior to that of her other colleagues. Josh could calculate complicated equations in his head and slice through other people's muddled thinking.

"As for happiness..." Marian shrugged one shoulder. "I attend the monthly meetings of the local Mensa chapter. You'd be surprised: they're a depressed, unsuccessful lot."

"I may be able to help you." Sharlene twisted the card in her purple-nailed fingers. "There may be a way around the ethics...although it won't be a love potion."

Marian's heart leaped with hope. "I'm interested."

"Instead of interfering with his free will, I'll work with yours. With your consent, I can make you attractive to him. He'll notice you in a different way from before. After that, it's up to him, and of course to you."

"How much?"

"Money won't help my child. What he needs is intelligence. And you have enough of that."

Marian laughed. "Intelligence can't be transferred."

"I believe it can. I know it can, if the circumstances are right."

"You want me to trade some of my intelligence for a love potion?" Marian laughed again, but the witch didn't join the chuckle.

"Give me 20 IQ points. They won't make any difference to your job, and they'll make a big difference to Daniel. With 20 points, Daniel will be able to learn how to use a toilet, and speak some simple words."

"If this magical procedure is possible, why don't you just give a hundred quid to some homeless drug addict? Many junkies would gladly trade their brains for a chance to shoot up."

"I tried!" The witch clasped her mug in both hands so hard that Marian thought it would break. "But any drug residue in the brain ruins the spell. Alcohol, too."

Even if this kind of magic was possible, it was preposterous. And yet...

"The totally sober people were the religious fanatics," the witch said. "And those won't get involved in magic. You say you don't do drink or drugs. It'll work with you, I can feel it. My intuition is never wrong."

"I don't think..." Marian reached for her briefcase.

"Listen to me, please. You're not frightened of witchcraft, or you wouldn't be here. And you have intelligence to spare. You have to help me!"

Marian stood. "I'm sorry, I..."

"I beg you, give Daniel a chance!" The witch reached across and clasped a hand around Marian's wrist. "If it doesn't work, what do you have to lose? Indulge a silly mother. And if it works... Think of Josh. Your soulmate, your true love, the man you're destined to be with. Isn't your love worth a try?"

Marian sat back down. This hypothetical spell was almost certainly doomed to failure, and she would lose nothing by giving it a try.

And if it worked - she would lose 20 IQ points. Would this be a problem?

She didn't need an IQ of 163. If anything, her exceptional intelligence was a hindrance to both success and happiness. With a more average IQ, she might have fared better in life, might have been more popular, enjoyed herself more.

And if it made her attractive to Josh. Josh... According to Jezebel.com, men avoided relationships with women whose intelligence trumped their own, so by lowering her IQ she would become more eligible as a serious partner. And if she could get those grey eyes to look at her, not just at the files she was showing him... If she could get his attention, then she could make him love her. The Stanford Binet was just a scale. Love was what mattered, that true, painful, pulsating love that yearned for its mate.

"How would it work?"

"You'll need to come back next time there's a new moon while Virgo is on the rise. Actually, today would be perfect, but we need a picture of him and something from his body."

"I have his photo," Marian said. "And a hair, will this work?" She always carried both with her. She drew the much-kissed photo from her wallet and unclasped the pillbox to extract the curled up hair she had picked from the back of his office chair last year, a blond treasure, strong and soft. "I have to get back to the office in half an hour."

"The ritual won't take long." Ms Shoenickle rose. "Are you sure you want this? That you are giving me a few drops of your blood by your own free will, that you want to be attractive to this one man?"

"I am."

"Very well." The witch drew the faded-edged curtains, dipping the place into darkness. She lit dozens of candles - fat stumps, marbled novelties in fancy holders and small tealights in vessels of painted glass. The glow of their clustered flickers sent tiny shadows dancing across the walls.

The witch dragged the table and one of the couches to the room's edge, waving away Marian's offer of assistance. In their place, she unrolled a large circular rug of black felt, painted with a five-pointed star in luminous green paint. She pointed at the rug. "Sit there."

Marian complied, tucked her legs to the side and pulled at the hem of her pencil skirt to keep her knees covered.

The witch carried equipment into the circle: an old-type bunsen burner, a dented copper cauldron, a sand-filled bowl, an assortment of glass jars and a workman's toolbox painted purple with mystic symbols in silver and gold.

With the kind of tongs other people use for sugar cubes, she held a charcoal disk over a candle flame until it glowed, then placed it on the sand and sprinkled translucent brown granules on it. They melted with a hiss, filling the air with sweet fumes.

"I'm casting the circle now. Don't move."

She picked up the glass-clad candles and placed them in a circle around the rug.

Then she loosened her frizzy hair and danced clockwise along the edge of the rug, waving her arms, shaking a rattle, and chanting incomprehensible syllables. Her earrings and bangles chinked with every move. Several times, the long swishing skirt hem brushed the candles but somehow didn't catch fire.

At last, she knelt in the circle, arms raised, and muttered what sounded like a sonorous prayer. Marian recognised the names of several Goddesses: Isis, Diana, Brigid, Astarte. Apparently Sharlene's was a mix & match religion, but the invocation seemed to do something, because the air prickled with what had to be magic.

The little hairs on the back of Marian's neck and arms rose as if from static. She kept still and watched as the witch lit the bunsen burner which started with a hiss, poured liquids from this flagon and that, sprinkled powdered herbs into the cauldron and stirred with a long-handled carved wooden spoon. The air took on a bitter, metallic tang.

The witch added the hair into the simmering concoction and waved Josh's photo through the cauldron's steam.

Then she picked up a black-handled knife and drew the blade through the burner's flame. "Your hand, please, dear."

She pricked Marian's middle finger with the tip of the knife, held it over the cauldron, and squeezed until red drops fell into the brew: One. Two. Three. Four. Nine drops altogether.

Marian pressed the cotton pad against her fingertip while Sharlene concluded the ritual with more cauldron stirring and chanting. She felt disoriented and a little dizzy, but that was probably the effect of the cauldron fumes.

At last, the witch danced around the circle once more, this time in the opposite direction, pinched out the flames and drew the curtains back.

"Have some more tea, dear, and a bite of gingerbread, to get you grounded." She took a big bite herself, and pushed the cake platter at Marian. "Grounding is important after a ritual, especially if you're not used to magic, and you're not, are you dear? It shouldn't take long for the effects to kick in, just a few hours. Are you meeting Josh tomorrow? Good. You'll notice a real difference."

"Thank you, Ms Shoenickle. I'll be in touch to report-"

"Call me Sharlene."

The boy started howling. "I have to take care of Daniel now. Take some flapjack with you, dear, why don't you? If I can help you further, give me a call." She fished a card from a velvet pouch and pressed it into Marian's hands. It read *Sharlene Ravenheart Shoenickle. Consultations by Appointment* in purple lettering. "Just remember: anything must be by your own free will."

*

The next day, Marian dressed with care: a blouse in feminine pink to ease the severity of her pinstripe suit, pearl earrings, a discreet touch of lipstick.

Perhaps the number-crunching took a little more effort than usual. Was this due to lack of sleep the night before, or had her IQ really dropped?

During her lunch break, instead of reading the *Financial Times* as usual, Marian took a "Discover Your IQ" test. Although less thorough than the exam administered by Mensa, it covered the same ground. The result: Marian's IQ was 143.

Discrepancies would arise from a variance of scales – Stanford-Binet versus Wechsler, for instance – and her brain's sleep-deprived exhaustion. But the difference was precisely 20 points.

The magic had worked. Did this mean she was now attractive to Josh?

She finished her salmon sandwich, opened the two top buttons of her blouse, dabbed on more Chanel No 5, and headed to Josh's office.

He looked up from the *Financial Times*. "Ah, Marian, come in." His eyes blinked, then widened. "Marian? How good to see you. You look... nice."

"Thank you." She perched on the chair next to him and caught a whiff of his scent: lemon, leather and a hint of sweat. Her heart pulsed in her chest.

Other women, with their superficial tastes, might not find Josh handsome: his shoulders too narrow for current fashions, his hairline receding already at thirty-two. But Marian saw the true beauty in the high forehead that housed a superior brain, the lines furrowed from deep thoughts, the silver glint in his slate-grey eyes.

She didn't dare meet his gaze, so she studied his hand instead, the tapering fingers, the manicured nails, yearning to clasp her own hand around his wrist where short blond hairs peeked out of the shirt cuff.

When she finally raised her eyes to his, she found his gaze lingering on her cleavage. Caught out, he blushed, looked away, fumbled with the pages of the *Financial Times*.

The spell was working! Josh found her attractive, and the result was worth every IQ point she had spent.

He pointed at the paper. "Do you think the sponsorship concept will make up for cuts in Arts Council funding?"

Not having read the article, she evaded. "Initial results may not be indicators of long-term effects. What's your take?"

His comments were well-reasoned as always, his articulation fluid, his voice steady and confident. After agreeing with his views, Marian was able to steer him to familiar topics, but she sensed that his attention was elsewhere. Her cleavage, she hoped. Perhaps she should buy a push-up bra.

At last, he cleared his throat. "I wonder if I may ask you for advice on... on a personal matter?"

"Sure." She gave him her most dazzling smile.

"The new chick in reception, the freckled blonde... How do I ask her out without making her feel pressured? I don't want her to think I'm one of those guys who use their rank for sexual harassment, and..." He shrugged. "You know what I mean."

Marian's throat constricted, and her hopes dropped to the bottom of her stomach. She managed to keep the smile plastered to her face. "Best you don't approach her in work hours," she counselled. "Wait until the Christmas office party. Things will be more relaxed, and you can make your move then."

If he waited until the Christmas do, this gave Marian two weeks to work her charms. "I didn't think she was your type. She's not that bright, is she?"

"What would I want a bright woman for?" For one ghastly moment, Marian thought he meant it, but then he laughed. "I'll do what you say. The Christmas party will be perfect. You're a pal, Marian."

When she left his office, the door clicked shut behind her. Her stomach churned with sour heat. Josh fancied her, that was clear. He just fancied someone else even more.

Josh, Josh. Why don't you see we're meant for each other, you and I? I love you, Josh. Josh, I love you. Josh, Josh, Josh.

You're a pal, he had said. A pal wasn't what she wanted to be, but there had been warmth in his voice, and his eyes had held that special silver glow.

She was so close to the winning line, but the receptionist was closer. With one week to outdo her rival, what could Marian do?

*

"How nice of you to visit," the witch gushed. "Come in. Join me for a cup of redbush tea."

Marian shook the water from her jacket and stepped into the warm, welcoming flat. Ambient music tinkled, and the air smelled of cinnamon and home-baked cake.

"I'm so grateful for what you've done," Sharlene jabbered on. "Daniel is learning to walk now, and he's painted this picture for me! Isn't it wonderful?"

Marian glanced at the random streaks of yellow and red which presumably meant that the kid was able to hold a crayon now, composed her face into a suitably admiring mask and made the required polite noises.

After urging her visitor to sample the organic spiced apple pie, Sharlene said, "And how are things with you? Has he come to appreciate your charms? Will there be an announcement soon?"

"That's why I'm here." Sharlene picked a pie crumb from her plate, ate it. "The spell definitely works - but not enough. I need more. Can you give me a little more attraction? Just a little. Five points worth."

The witch stirred honey into her tea so intently that the spoon clinked in the cup. At last, her chin came up. "Twenty."

"I don't need that much, and I'm not willing to..."

"Twenty or nothing." Sharlene's face was hard. "Your choice."

Marian's stomach tightened. That would reduce her IQ to 123. Still far above the average population; still above almost everyone working at Groneagle, and certainly more than that bimbo at reception. But what a humiliating drop from 163!

The emptiness in the pit of the stomach felt like it was going to shrivel and consume her entire body from the inside.

Love or IQ? IQ or love? Josh, Josh, Josh, I need you so much! If you knew how much I'm suffering for you, would you rush here and rescue me?

Pride warred against need, and lost. "I'll do it."

"By your own free will?"

Marian lifted the table. "By my own free will."

*

The office Christmas party came, and Marian wore a new dress in shimmering pink satin – Josh liked pink; he had admired her in that pink blouse – strapless and covered in sequins. She stood out from the other women in their standard little black dresses like a butterfly amidst moths. She drew a lot of attention from her male colleagues. Even the old grumpy ones asked her to dance.

At last, Josh joined her. "You look stunning tonight, Marian," he said. "This is quite some dress you're wearing. I didn't think you had it in you."

Her heart did a crazy, joyful leap.

They danced, and he held her closer than necessary, his warm hand softly brushing the bare skin on her back. He had a wonderful sense of rhythm. Marian's mind buzzed with giddy hope. This happy, dizzy lightness must be how it felt to be tipsy with champagne.

For an hour they talked – comparing formalist and structural approaches to the criticism of epistolary literature, discussing the extent to which post-impressionist paintings were rooted in the Salon des Refusés, and the interpretation of Greek myth in operas of the seventeenth century. At the same time, her throat burned with the words she couldn't say: *I love you, Josh. Josh, I love you.* She kept them back: it was too soon.

Her heart performed a wild dance of hope. He was gazing at her with such intensity, his grey eyes so caressing, so earnest, so soft! And he smelled good – an Italian cologne, she guessed, that blended with his natural scent of lemon and leather. She was glad she had changed her perfume to the bolder Boudoir. *I love you, Josh. And you love me. Can't you feel it yet?*

She wanted to ruffle his hair, to cover his neck with kisses, to cool her burning palms on his skin.

Eventually, raising his glass to hers, he said, "Time to mingle, or people will talk."

His eyes held amusement tinged with regret. He was right, of course, perceptive as always, gauging the situation just right.

Marian assented with a light heart. They had clicked. All was well now. They could afford to be separated for an hour to meet the conventions of an office Christmas do.

She chatted, danced and declined several vulgar propositions.

It was past midnight when she saw that Josh was doing more than talk. The way he was holding that leggy marketing brunette for the dance... his hand was practically clasping her buttock.

Disbelief, then pain stabbed at her heart. She told herself firmly it meant nothing. It wasn't the receptionist bimbo, just a sexy female who happened to throw herself at him. Perhaps he had drunk alcohol and didn't know what he was doing. Besides, they weren't engaged yet, hadn't even kissed or exchanged commitments; he still had the right to enjoy a flirtation. Perhaps he was even doing this deliberately, to distract the gossips. Besides, he couldn't really enjoy talking with her: that girl didn't know Monet from Manet or Orpheus from Morpheus.

But it didn't help. The way his lips brushed the brunette locks, the way his hand dipped into the low back of that black dress, the way he laughed with her giggles... it hurt like a dozen knives slicing at Marian's insides.

*

Once again, Marian rang the bell of *Sharlene Ravenheart Shoenickle, Consultations by Appointment*.

"Come in, come in," Sharlene urged. "I have wonderful news. Daniel is improving so much, thanks to you. Every IQ point you've donated, he's gained at least two. He gets private tutoring now, and will start mainstream school after the Christmas break." She ushered her into the living room and poured tea. "And how are things with you? Has Josh proposed?"

"He's so close! But he needs a little more help. Could you... just once more?" Without sitting down for tea, Marian strode to the place of magic and lifted the table.

Sharlene frowned. "With another 20 points, Daniel be bright enough catch up on his delayed development, and that would be simply wonderful. But are you sure this is what you want? It may impair your ability to do your job."

With a jerk of her chin, Marian dismissed that concern. "They don't appreciate me at work anyway. After all I've done for Groneagle & Co, all the major developments, they berate me for the slightest mistakes." Those weren't even major errors, just small things that had nothing to do with intelligence, just the management's petty mindset. "I'm thinking of quitting. What's a job, compared with love? Can you give me awesome boobs? Josh likes boobs."

"I can't change your body shape, but I can put a glamour on your chest - as long as it's your own free will."

In reply, Marian carried the table and the couch out of the way, while Sharlene lit the candles and fetched the rug.

*

At the department meeting, Josh's gaze was glued to Marian's cleavage, displayed in a new sparkly halterneck. She pulled the fabric further down to treat him to an extended view. His eyes nearly popped out.

Judging by his wide eyes and the way he moistened his lips and frequently smoothed his hair, he wasn't paying no more attention to the manager's droning than she was.

Afterwards, he suggested they meet in the cafeteria over lunch to discuss the project further.

She took care to lean forward a little while sipping her coffee, to give him a good view, which he clearly appreciated, and a whiff of Boudoir. But when she brushed her leg against his, a brief flush coloured his face. His leg pulled away, his gaze focused on his cod fillet with mushy peas, and he talked without pause about development budgets and amortising overheads.

When she ran the tip of her tongue across her lips the way she had seen seductive women do in the movies, he gathered his briefcase. "Time to get back to work."

*

"I want to trade more IQ points," Marian announced. "But this time it has to work."

"I can enhance your erotic allure further." Sharlene tilted her head. "Daniel could do with more brightness, although he's doing much better now, and each point you've donated seems to have converted to more than one for him."

She drew the curtains, shutting out the light. "But I have to ask this. Are you really willing to lessen your intelligence? Are you certain it's what you want? You'll be the most physically attractive woman in the world for Josh - but if he values you for your brains..."

"I don't want him to value me for my brains!" Marian stomped a foot on the rug with impatience. "Do you know where that leads? I've been there, and it leads nowhere at all. All the while I was Groneagle's most intelligent employee, he treated me like I was a sophisticated computer. At least, now he sees me as a woman. I need a man for love, not work. I don't want him to talk about amortising overheads; I get enough of that at the job."

"Let's do a smaller trade. How about ten points worth of IQ and allure? It may be enough to hook your man."

"I don't want a 'maybe', I want him definitely mad with lust. I want Josh to touch me, to take me to bed, to kiss me out of my mind."

"He'll want to take you to bed. He'll want it very much," Sharlene promised. "But whether he acts on his desire or not, that's up to him. The magic won't interfere with his free will."

"So start the ritual already. Ten IQ points, or however many it takes. Make me so sexy he can't resist. It's my own free will."

*

The next morning, Marian's employment was terminated. The arrangement was amicable: Groneagle gave time off work in lieu of notice so she could leave at once, and paid a generous compensation.

Plastering her face with determined cheer as a shield against her colleagues' pitying stares, she spent an hour clearing her cubicle, packing her supply of biscuits, wiping personal details from the computer, carrying stacks of financial papers to the recycling bin. In her mind, relief mingled with regret. This had been her workplace for almost five years - years of stimulation and ambition, of exciting discoveries and of drudgery, of gaining insights for Groneagle and recognition for herself.

Would she miss it sometimes? She tossed sheets of scribbled notes into the shredder. Of course she wouldn't miss this tiny cubicle in the airless office, nor the computer that crashed at crucial moments, the constant hum and beep of printers and phones, the invasive chatter of the secretaries, and the stuck-up directors who didn't understand the value of her work. It was time for a change. Maybe she would do something completely different for a while before deciding on her next major career move.

A cluster of colleagues gathered at pub for a farewell lunch, their faces painted with embarrassment and curiosity. Josh, looking oh-so-handsome in his grey suit with the silver tie that matched his sadness-filled eyes, raised his pint glass. "We'll all miss you, Marian."

Of course what he meant to say was "I'll miss you, Marian, I'll be devastated when you're gone," but he couldn't say that with the whole office listening in. So she sent him a conspiratorial smile that said she understood and promised to keep her love for him.

"Let's keep in touch," he said, with a warm smile that caressed her figure.

Now she'd left Groneagle, they'd be able to meet without concerns about what people might think. Happiness was hers at last.

*

Finding a temp job was easy, although operating the checkout till was more challenging than people imagined.

Twice a day, she texted Josh, sending him photos of herself. He liked the pictures - especially the one in the sequinned pink bikini - and asked to see more. She checked every hour for new messages. At night, she lay in bed, clad in nothing but a spritz of Boudoir, rereading his texts over and over, imagining his body entwined with hers. Soon it would be true.

*

When Josh received an award for outstanding contributions to financial research, he invited her to the ceremony. "You had part in that research," the note said in his firm, masculine handwriting. "I couldn't have done it without you."

She pressed her lips on his signature and inhaled from the card, eager to detect a trace of his scent.

For hours, she tried on outfits in front of the mirror. Nothing was good enough, sexy enough, not even the three slinky numbers she had bought especially for the occasion. At last, she settled on a dress in shiny cerise PVC that zipped from hem to cleavage at the front.

This was what she would wear when he finally took her home. She rehearsed unzipping it so she would get her striptease just right.

High-heeled slingbacks, long acrylic nails and a cerise lipstick called Moist Love completed the look.

As soon as she entered the room, she knew the dress was the right choice. Mouths opened, eyes blinked.

Marian found Josh talking to the Groneagle's director of finance. From his unsmiling face, she could tell that he was bored, so she hooked her arm around his and drew him away.

He was wearing a charcoal suit with a white shirt and the silver-grey waistcoat she liked so much. How sweet of him to dress up for her!

While she waited for him to bring her the requested orange juice, she drew the zipper a few notches lower, bearing enough cleavage to show she wasn't wearing a bra. When he returned, he stared at her cleavage, so entranced he forgot his drink.

Marian emptied her own glass, then took his from his hand and placed them both on the tray of a passing waiter. Then she squeezed herself against him. Ah, he smelled so good! Lemon and leather again. Her own body heat would release the scent of Boudoir.

With her ear pressed against his shoulder, she could hear his rapid heart and feel the rising of his chest as his breath quickened.

"No, Marian," he whispered. "This isn't the time and place." But while his mouth said "no" his eyes said "yes," and even as his hands pushed her gently away, they lingered for a moment on her arms, warm and soft and full of meaning.

He withdrew to talk to that boring finance guy again, and some former colleagues tried to draw Marian into a chat about numbers and computers. She couldn't wait to get away from them.

She kept throwing meaningful glances at Josh's direction, and he was frequently looking her way, too.

At last, Josh made some excuse and joined her. "Shall we go for a breath of air?"

He led her into the garden, but they soon tired of gazing at the stars and the winter-bare flowerbeds, so they returned indoors.

In an alcove near the back door, hidden from curious onlookers, he kissed her. Oh, what a kiss! His lips were warm and dry, soft and firm, tender and hungry and wonderful.

His hand slid up her bare arms to her front, where they fondled her breasts through the PVC. Under his fingers' tender greed, her nipples sprang to life, demanding more, more, more.

"You're so beautiful, Marian," he panted, his voice hoarse with shared need.

Happiness pulsed in her blood. It felt so good. But she wanted more - she wanted commitment. She wanted him to want only her. "Josh...." she moaned.

Josh released her. "We'll do more of this later, yes?"

"Now," she begged, sliding her hand down his abdomen and into the waistband.

He cleared his throat and pulled away. "Later."

For the rest of the ceremony, he didn't even look at her, however much she tried to catch his eye with seductive wiggles of her hips. Instead, he talked with the finance director, the human resources manager, and some other bigwigs who seemed to think they owned him just because they paid his salary.

Drastic action was called for.

She stepped in front of him, ratched the zip open. She hadn't planned to give the finance director a glimpse of her show, but other than that, it went as smoothly as she had rehearsed it.

Josh gasped.

Now she had his attention. It also showed everyone in the room that they were lovers. With their relationship acknowledged, he would no longer need to hide what was between them.

He drew away. "Are you drunk? For pity's sake, Marian, pull yourself together."

"I never drink, you know that."

He was shy, but the silver glint of love shone in his eyes. All he needed was a little encouragement.

She stepped out of her dress, spun it on her finger, and draped it around his neck. "Josh," she purred.

Someone jerked her arm on her back. A male voice hissed, "Security, ma'am. Please come with me."

Regret painted Josh's face, but he made no move to help her as the uniformed thug pulled her to the door. He just called out, "Put her in a taxi home. I'll pay."

Rejection churned with cruel pain. Clearly, she needed to up her level of lure. The witch had lied when she said ten points would be enough. She needed more: another ten points, or twenty or thirty, whatever it took to drive Josh out of his mind with wanting.

*

Dusting bookshelves was tricky. Marian had to make sure every shelf was clean, and not knock any of the figures over. Her boss was a witch who had a very clever son. He would start college soon although he was only fourteen. On the shelf was a photo of him looking proud.

Marian had a photo in her pocket. She pulled it out. It was sticky and stained but she pressed her lips on it. This was her true love. His name was Josh, and he had kissed her for real.

*

Josh gazed at his new bride with pride and love. Most men would not find Annabel beautiful, with her boyish-slender body and her mousy curls. But she was the kind of woman he had searched for all his life, and had sometimes despaired if she even existed. He was blessed to have finally found her: A woman who was his intellectual equal.

EXCERPT FROM THE DARK EPIC FANTASY NOVEL STORM DANCER

Merida is a magician who can change the weather with her dance. Her government sends her on a mercy mission to bring rain to a faraway land gripped by drought and starvation. But when she arrives, she finds the terms of the contract have not been met, and the conditions not right for the magic. The ritual requires certain planets to align, but the ruler has changed the date to coincide with a national festival. She needs a specific location where two rivers meet; instead, she has to perform in an arena as part of the public entertainment. She expected a well-rehearsed orchestra to play a specific tune; instead, she gets two drummers who've never heard the music. How can she work magic under these conditions?

The sun stood three finger-breaths above the horizon, painting the arena in soft gold.

When five green-clad courtiers escorted Merida into the arena, the spectators rose from their seats to cheer as if she were a favourite entertainer. The stone idols of the Mighty Ones seemed to watch as she skirted around the dark patches of dried blood. Her white trousers shimmered against yellowed grass, but the ground under her feet contained no earth magic. Not the faintest tingling reached her bare soles.

Wood was stacked for four equal walls of flames higher than any Merida had worked with, but even this would not suffice to draw much rain, not with the moon in the wrong phase, the planets in a pointless place, and the earth's pulse lacking.

Doum-tek doumtek doum-tek doumtek. Merida cast a quick glance at the two green-uniformed men squatting under a striped awning, drums in their laps. At least they had mastered the rhythm, and what they lacked in refinement, they made up in fervency. The acoustics were strong, and the sound carried. But two drums were not enough.

She needed another source. All around her, voices cheered, hands clapped, feet stomped. People. Human energy. Forbidden fuel. Merida had never broken the magicians' code of ethics, never fed on people power. But if she could not draw rain, Kirral would smirk, and she would have to return to Riverland with her head bowed.

She glanced at the rows of excited spectators, sensed plenty of power waiting to be tapped, and wished she could assess its quantity. To make sure, she had better go even higher into trance, not just to fourth level but to fifth.

She climbed the platform in the centre of the firewood square, and spoke the required homage to the four Virtues, as expected from an accredited member of a school of magic. She performed a quick but intense sequence from the Disciplined Path, stroking her own aura and kicking an imaginary foe, and chanted to focus her magic.

The vibrations from the applause caressed her bare arms, her cheeks, tingled through her body's fibres. Resolutely, Merida opened herself up. She allowed the forbidden fuel to flow into her abdomen like liquid into a bowl. She felt her flesh heat and her strength grow. Already her own silver aura buzzed around her skin.

Greenbelts set their torches to the wood. Flames shot up. Now it was too late to back away. She was trapped by the dancing tongues. Smoke scratched her nostrils, and heat bathed her skin.

All she could do was to pull her fear of fire inside her, stir it into positive energy, and focus on her task. She raised her arms to the sky to call for rain. She tossed her head, her shoulders, her body, releasing magic.

Doum-tek doumtek, doum-tek doumtek.

Five thousand people in the audience clapped the rhythm. The liquid strength of the crowd's support surged through her. They wanted the rain, and were willing her to succeed. She drank their appreciation and turned it to power. Her heartflame heated and fuelled her dance.

She surrendered all control to the pulsing of the drums. *Doum-tek doumtek, doum-tek doumtek.* Her arms rose high on one side, then collapsed in the front. The momentum carried her arms up to the other side, her chest and head followed. Sparks of magic crackled in her hair.

She rose easily through the two ordinary levels of trance into the third at which she normally worked major large magic. Then she climbed to the fourth, the dangerous fifth. Power soared through her, sent her blood singing. Weight drained from her body, consciousness seeped away. Almost without effort, she rose to the sixth level, the one no magician had achieved since Helva Hein.

Her mind was lightness, riding inside a cloud-powered bliss. She stirred her inner cauldron, drew the magic through her heart into her head, and contacted the element of rain.

A long time passed before her hands quivered in response. Water had heard her call; now she had to attract it. She pulled the rain clouds she could not yet see. So much power pumped through her blood, she knew she had enough to bring rain, but she wanted more, more, more. Enough water to sate the earth, enough to wipe the smirk off the Consort's face.

Excited cheers greeted the first purple cloud on the horizon.

Then the first raindrops fell on her naked arms, big drops, warm and soft. Shouts of joy and hissing flames nearly drowned out the drumbeats, but she kept going.

The rain poured harder, drowning the flames.

She danced, and danced, and danced. She climbed into further levels of trance, raising yet more energy, calling yet more rain. Her white tunic had lost all substance, a thin textile film glued to her skin.

Violent water crashed on empty white stone steps, ran in streams and cascaded down the corridors into the grass arena.

The cheering spectators cowered under parasols, and eventually left for better shelter in the town. Only the drummers stayed under their feeble awning. Merida dropped to a lower trance to observe them. The descent made her ears ring so loud they almost burst. When drum skins dampened and the sounds dulled, they kept the rhythm going by clapping their hands. Their stamina matched hers.

Doum-tek, doumtek. Doum-tek, doumtek.

Greyness descended, then night-black. Time to stop. She had won. Now was the time to celebrate the joys of victory. After signalling the drummers to slow, she braced herself. As she plummeted into the lower levels, a dizzy void replaced her spent strength, and she collapsed in happy exhaustion.

*

Servants bustled her into a litter. Once at the palace, tiredness ripped Merida's mind to shreds. In her rush to ready herself, she had not prepared proper aftercare. No honey-water waited to restore energy, no hot brick warmed her bed.

When greenbelts supported her arms on both sides, she was too shattered to resent the touch. They guided her not to the dormitory, but to the palace's audience hall. She needed rest, dry clothes, nourishment, but was too weak to protest. Disoriented and shivering with cold, she dropped into the chair. At least the armrests were wood. Wood energy, though weak, was easy to absorb.

Teruma draped a wool cloak over her.

She could barely hear the Consort's speech of thanks, let alone enjoy her triumph, or compose a formal reply. With effort, she turned the corners of her mouth upwards.

The Queen, fat and stately beside her Consort, spoke. "You will stay in the Queendom, our guest forever."

Merida's mind jerked awake. "No... honoured... some days, then Riverland. Home."

The Consort slapped his thigh. "You will stay in Quislak. If not as a guest, then as part of my harem."

What a bizarre Quislaki custom to express formal gratitude by proposing marriage. Searching for the appropriate phrase, she struggled for strength to speak. "...honoured... regret... return to Riverland."

Sleep. She needed sleep.

"You misunderstood." Teruma said on her left. "You'll be a wife whether you want to or not."

"No," Merida croaked.

Reality and nightmares swam together in her head. She heard Kirral's voice from a distance. "We shall dispense with the traditional rites for the occasion."

Virtues help me, help me, Merida pleaded, but she was too feeble to focus. The room spun. Clutching the armrests, she sought to rally what energy she could muster. Her belly cauldron was a hollow vessel, her heartflame a faint spark. Summoning droplets of strength, she pulled herself up and dropped at the Queen's feet.

"I beg you, Ma'am. Help me."

"I do not involve myself in my husband's harem affairs." The Queen yawned and clapped twice. Greenbelts dragged Merida back to her seat.

"I demand…" She tried to shout, but it came out as a croak. "… speak regular ambassador."

"Quislak no longer has a Riverian ambassador. Diplomatic relations are severed." The Consort held Merida's pass and accreditation over the incense burner.

Her power spent, she could not stop him. Slow-licking flames devoured the precious parchments.

"I … no more magic… never… for you."

"We have ways to make you." Kirral smirked. "Besides, I have other uses for you."

FURTHER READING

This book teaches you how to write about magic. If you want to find out about the history of magic, a specific Magic System, detailed spellcraft techniques or how to become a magician yourself, many interesting books are available to help you in your quest. Here are some book suggestions to get you started.

MAGIC SYSTEMS

Ancient Egyptian Magic by Bob Brier

Liber Null & Psychonaut: An Introduction to Chaos Magic by Peter J. Carroll

Italian Witchcraft: The Old Religion of Southern Europe by Raven Grimassi

Book of Shadows: A Modern Woman's Journey Into the wisdom of witchcraft by Phyllis Curott

What Witches Do by Stewart Farrar

Hedge Witch: A Guide to Solitary Witchcraft by Rae Beth

Witchcraft: A Beginner's Guide by Teresa Morey

Ancient Christian Magic by Marvin W. Meyer and Richard Smith

Spiritual and Demonic Magic: From Ficino to Campanella by D. P. Walker

Magic of the Celtic Otherworld: Irish History, Lore & Rituals by Stephen Blamires

Forbidden Rites: A Necromancer's Manual of the Fifteenth Century by Richard Kieckhefer

Communing with the Spirits: The Magical Practice of Necromancy by Martin Coleman

Greek and Roman Necromancy by Daniel Ogden

Great Book of Magical Art, Hindu Magic and East Indian Occultism & The Book of Secret Hindu, Ceremonial, and Talismanic Magic by L. W. de Laurence

Northern Magic: Rune Mysteries and Shamanism by Edred Thorsson

Sympathetic Magic Of The Ainu - The Native People Of Japan by John Batchelor

Gypsy Magic: A Romany Book of Spells, Charms, and Fortune-Telling by Patrinella Cooper

The Druid Magic Handbook: Ritual Magic Rooted in the Living Earth by John Michael Greer and David Spangler

The Voodoo Hoodoo Spellbook by Denise Alvarado and Doktor Snake

The Keys to the Gateway of Magic: Summoning the Solomonic Archangels and Demon Princes (a 17th century book, edited by Stephen Skinner and David Rankine)

Nocturnicon by Konstantinos

Enochian Vision Magick by Lon Duquette

Simplified Qabala Magic by Ted Andrews

Fire in the Head: Shamanism and the Celtic Spirit by Tom Cowan

Of Water and the Spirit: Ritual, Magic and Initiation in the Life of an African Shaman by Malidoma Patrice Some

Ceremonial Magic: A Guide to the Mechanisms of Ritual by Israel Regardie

Magic and Alchemy by Rosemary Ellen Guiley

The 21 Lessons of Merlyn A study in Druid Magic and Lore by Douglas Monroe

Scottish Witchcraft: The History and Magick of the Picts by Raymond Buckland

Ancient Jewish Magic: A History by Gideon Bohak

Santeria: African Magic in Latin America by Migene Gonzalez-Wippler

The Complete Idiot's Guide to Alchemy by Dennis William Hauck

High Magic: Theory & Practice by Frater U.:D.:

Condensed Chaos: An Introduction to Chaos Magic by Phil Hine

TECHNIQUES, TOOLS, INGREDIENTS, SPELLS, RITUALS

Cunningham's Encyclopedia of Magical Herbs by Scott Cunningham

Cunningham's Encyclopedia of Crystal, Gem & Metal Magic by Scott Cunningham

Earth Power: Techniques of Natural Magic by Scott Cunningham

Earth, Air, Fire, and Water: More Techniques of Natural Magic by Scott Cunningham

Celtic Sex Magic: For Couples, Groups, and Solitary Practitioners by Jon G. Hughes

Modern Sex Magick: Secrets of Erotic Spirituality by Donald Michael Kraig

Magic's in the Bag: Creating Spellbinding Gris Gris Bags & Sachets by Jude Bradley and Cheré Dastugue Coen

Composing Magic: How to Create Magical Spells, Rituals, Blessings, Chants, and Prayers by Elizabeth Barrette

Death and Destruction: How to Cast Magic Spells for Vengeance, Harm, &c. by Talia Felix

Voodoo Dolls In Magick And Ritual by Denise Alvarado

Protection and Reversal Magick (Beyond 101) by Jason Miller

Practical Candleburning Rituals: Spells and Rituals for Every Purpose by Raymond Buckland

Amulets & Talismans for Beginners: How to Choose, Make & Use Magical Objects by Richard Webster

Herb Magic for Beginners by Ellen Dugan

Futhark: A Handbook of Rune Magic by Edred Thorsson

Crystal Enchantments: A Complete Guide to Stones and Their Magical Properties by D.J. Conway and Brian Ed. Conway

PowerSpells: Get the Magical Edge in Business, Work Relationships, and Life by Lexa Roséan

Creating Magical Tools: The Magician's Craft by Chic Cicero and Sandra Tabatha Cicero

Encyclopedia of 5,000 Spells by Judika Illes

Love Magic by Laurie Cabot

Body Guards: Protective Amulets & Charms by Desmond Morris

Llewellyn's Complete Book of Correspondences: A Comprehensive & Cross-Referenced Resource for Pagans & Wiccans by Sandra Kynes

Hoodoo Herb and Root Magic: A Materia Magica of African-American Conjure by Catherine Yronwode

Practical Protection Magick: Guarding & Reclaiming Your Power by Ellen Dugan

Money Magic: Mastering Prosperity in its True Element by Frater U.:D.:

Brain Magick: Exercises in Meta-Magick and Invocation by Philip H. Farber

Financial Sorcery: Magical Strategies to Create Real and Lasting Wealth by Jason Miller

Everyday Witch A to Z Spellbook: Wonderfully Witchy Blessings, Charms & Spells by Deborah Blake

Practical Sigil Magic: Creating Personal Symbols for Success by Frater U.:D.:

HISTORY, SOCIETY, PSYCHOLOGY

Magic, Mystery, and Science: The Occult in Western Civilization by Danny Ethus Burton and David A. Grandy

Magic in the Roman World: Pagans, Jews and Christians by Naomi Janowitz

The History of Magic by Eliphas Levi

Magic: A History of Its Rites, Rituals, and Mysteries (Dover Occult) by Eliphas Levi and A. E. Waite

Heresy, Magic and Witchcraft in Early Modern Europe by Gary K. Waite

Grimoires: A History of Magic Books by Owen Davies

History of Magic and the Occult by Kurt Selegmann

Magic in the Ancient World by Fritz Graf and Franklin Philip

Magic in the Middle Ages by Richard Kieckhefer

Believing in Magic: The Psychology of Superstition by Stuart A. Vyse (May 18, 2000)

DEAR READER

I hope you've enjoyed this book and gained many practical ideas for your writing. If you found it helpful, I'll be thrilled if you post a review on Amazon, Barnes&Noble, BookLikes, GoodReads, or wherever you purchased it or are a member.

If you email me the URL to your review, I'll send you a free review copy (ebook) of one of my other Writer's Craft books: *Writing Scary Scenes, Writing Fight Scenes, The Word-Loss Diet, Writing About Villains, Writing Short Stories to Promote Your Novels, Writing Dark Stories, Twitter for Writers, Why Does My Book Not Sell? 20 Simple Fixes, Writing Vivid Settings.*

Let me know if you've found any errors, omissions, broken links or typos in this book, please let me know. Some errors always sneak past the eagle eyes of the proofreaders. Also contact me if you have questions. My email is **rayne_hall_author@yahoo.com**. I look forward to hearing from you.

Perhaps you know other writers who might benefit from this book? Tell them about it.

On Twitter, you can follow me @RayneHall. **https://twitter.com/RayneHall** I'm very active on Twitter; it's my preferred social network. If you tweet that you've read this book, I'll follow you back – though you may have to remind me, because I have many followers and it's easy to miss a tweet.

Rayne Hall

Printed in Great Britain
by Amazon